# Racism and anti-Racism in the world: before and after 1945

Author: Kathleen Brush

ISBN: 978-0-9828823-5-1

## Before we begin

Recently, thousands have said they were unproud to be American because of its racism? I hope this book will show that America is an anti-racist leader, and this is something to be proud of.

To George R. Brush Jr. and to all American military personnel who risked their lives so America and Americans could and can be free, American slaves could be free, and people all over the world of all colors and creeds had the chance to be free.

A special thanks to P.T. Caso, Cregan Howard (1944-2020), Dr. Michael Triolo, Bruce Coleman, John Bianchi and Boots Caso for their unvarnished input on how improve this booklet.

**This book was updated on December 7, 2020.**

# Table of Contents

# INTRODUCTION

Nineteen-forty-five was a global tipping point. Instead of nations being routinely racist, they were to be anti-racist. The long era of *laissez faire* attitudes toward discrimination was officially ending. One of history's evilest men, Hitler, prompted something good -- an unambiguous wake-up call that stratifying populations as inferior and superior was horribly wrong.

Evil though had to be bested by good. This was the role of American President Franklin Delano Roosevelt (FDR). FDR was a relentless champion of creating a unified global organization that would end discrimination. His success lie in parlaying American victory in WWII to get the support of global powers to create the United Nations (UN) in 1945. People would now be given the right to self-determine nationhood. The subjugation of blacks and Asians to whites in Africa and Asia was being abolished. To end discrimination within states, nations had to commit to delivering fundamental freedoms[1] to all people.

The right to determine nationhood prompted mammoth change. In 1945 there was a handful of empires and 53 nations. In 2020, there were zero empires and 193 nations. Ending discrimination would similarly prompt monstrous change. For millennia, the unequal allocation of freedoms and privilege was how polities brought order to diverse populations. But this was not to be the way forward.

Several things quickly became clear: many national leaders were at best committing to a utopian ideal; most leaders, just like the predecessor imperial rulers, didn't see discrimination as a problem, but rather a solution; what some saw as depraved indifferences to human life, others saw as a sovereign right; and a handful of nations were committing to anti-racism. These were the world's first woke nations.

Seventy-five years later, these anti-racist nations have become familiar with the complexities of ending discrimination. Governments can only do so much. They have legal systems that give them the power to end institutional discrimination. But they do not have the power to stop parents, journalists, commentators, teachers and different leaders that purposely or inadvertently teach and reinforce discrimination. They cannot address perceptions of discrimination that deviate from reality, they cannot force integration, they cannot cancel history, they cannot stop people from saying mean things, and they are unsuited to address unconscious discrimination.[2] People of any color or religion, even those that believe they are egalitarian, host a range of unconscious biases.[3] Governments can enforce what you can't do within the

---

[1] According to the UN's International Covenant on Civil and Political Rights, fundamental freedoms include but are not limited to freedom of religion and speech, protection from exploitation and arbitrary actions of the state, and a right to education.

[2] When it became illegal to discriminate against people based on race, religion, sex, or national origin, overt discrimination was curtailed but unconscious discrimination/bias increased.

[3] Unconscious biases stem from stereotypes. People hold stereotypes of different people, for example, whites are privileged and racist, blacks are dangerous and lazy, Latinos can't be trusted, Asians think they are superior, Muslims are terrorists, and Jews are greedy. A person that prides themselves on being egalitarian can unconsciously hold racial stereotypes that can result in unconsciously seeing white

bounds of enumerated and implied rights, but they cannot enforce what you can and cannot think consciously or unconsciously.

The objective of this book is to raise awareness to the origins and evolution of diversity, discrimination, and anti-discrimination in societies all over the world before and after 1945. It should become evident that prior to 1945 formally or informally stratifying, segregating, and cleansing populations were normal ways to order societies. In 1945, a stake was laid in the ground. Viewing populations as superior and inferior was amoral, and all 193 nations have signed the UN Charter indicating agreement. However, only a small subset of nations has endeavored to honor this commitment.

America was at the fore in 1945. It became the first nation to establish an anti-racist legal system, and then the first nation with a private sector demonstrably committed to anti-racism. It remains at the fore of the demonstrably anti-racist nations. Anti-racist nations have shown how extraordinarily complex it is to end discriminatory beliefs rooted in history and perpetuated at home, communities, and generally in society. But the fight is young and none of the anti-racist nations are giving up, meanwhile others won't even enter the ring. Most nations are demonstrably and unapologetically racist; they see real value in homogenous societies, ordered societies, and privileged and unprivileged people.

## Diversity & Discrimination: Origins & Evolution

It can seem a shocking revelation that Chinese, Russian, Islamic, and European empires were still competing for global supremacy in the early 20th century. This was the Era of Empires (1453-1945). Five hundred years of competing transformed the world. Instead of three populous connected continents, there were six. Instead of indigenous religions being pervasive, Christianity and Islam had religious majorities in 83% of the countries of the world. Instead of a tower of babel, most people spoke one of nine empire languages as a first or second language. Instead of ethnically and religiously homogenous societies, the world consisted of ethnically and religiously heterogeneous societies.

When the era began, Asians lived in Asia, whites lived in Europe, and blacks lived in Africa. The three New World continents (North America, Oceania, and South America) had relatively small indigenous populations. During the era, diversity skyrocketed from: empires conquering diverse people; tens of millions freely or forcibly traveling to foreign lands to escape religious persecution, or to work or serve prison sentences; government policies; and the creation and re-creation of colonial borders. These empires functioned like global population mixers. In some colonies, populations became overt composites of descendants from Africa, the Americas, Asia, and Europe. They were not, however composites of equals. Discrimination was omnipresent, because this was how diversity was managed.

people as arrogant, be uncomfortable in the presence of blacks and Muslims, distrust Latinos and Jews, and be skeptical of claims by Asians.

Populations everywhere were officially or unofficially socially stratified in an order of descending privilege. Social hierarchies baked privilege and discrimination into societal foundations. However, when empires conquered lands, hierarchies were turned upside down. The race and religion of the conquerors was on top, and the indigenous majority was below. The alteration of social hierarchies following conquest was one reason wars of conquest could be so bloody. There was plenty to lose, like land, freedoms and privilege. But, once the conquest was complete, accepting a new designated station in life was the least bad option.

Social hierarchies were not the only means to discriminatorily manage populations. There were massacres, segregations, expulsions, forced emigration, enslavement, indentured servitude that resembled slavery, genocides, population transport, ethnic cleansing, assorted privileges for some and restrictions for others.

In this time, none of this was called discrimination; it was called social ordering and ordered societies were believed to be key to social peace.[4] Today, many would call these practices heinous, racist, intolerant, elitist, arrogant, sexist, and illegal. History is like that; it never measures up to the modern standards that come from change. But what are the global modern standards for non-discriminatory societies? There are none. Many nations have not modernized their views on discrimination. They like their societies ordered.

Excluding pervasive inequalities that accompanied stratification, no discriminatory practice affected more people than slavery. Enslaving people following wars of conquest was a traditional behavior throughout history and it continued into the 21st century. Slavery, in general, was legal and common before and during the Era of Empire.[5] It counts among history's highly regrettable traditional behaviors. Even more regrettable, slavery continues into the present. But it is no longer seen as just another way to make money, and it no longer takes the forms of having global feeder systems, friends and family selling friends and family, ordinary people engaged in kidnapping, entire economies built on slavery, slave industries employing people from all over the world and attracting thousands of investors, and Muslim pirates, privateers and African leaders carrying out thousands of conquests and raids specifically to sell the conquered and at times simultaneously expel their opponents.[6] All of the above were motivated by the rewards from meeting demands driven by African, European, and Arab slave traders and their clients.[7]

Empire-defined borders also introduced diversity. At the start of the Era of Empire, boundaries were as fluid as a polity's ability to defend them. Loosely defined borders generally enclosed small territories of homogenous populations. The

---

[4] The first application of discrimination as a term indicating unequal treatment of diverse people was in the United States in the 19th century.

[5] In the empires controlling most of the world, the abolition of slavery only gained some momentum after the French Revolution (1799). (France reinstated slavery in its colonies between 1802 and 1848.) There was greater momentum to end slavery in the 20th century. The last nation to abolish slavery was Mauritania in 1981. In 2020 slavery is still not a criminal offense in 94 nations.

[6] Some articles mention raids by whites, but there are no specifics. There is agreement that it was near impossible for whites to conduct slave raids in Africa.

[7] So grand were the trades in slaves that descendants of African slaves became the majority or significant minority populations in dozens of nations in the Americas. The same was not true in the lands served by the Arab slave trade. Although this trade enslaved more and endured longer than the Atlantic trade, measures were taken to limit the growth of black populations.

empires changed this. With little regard for the final composition of communities, and any histories of ethnic or religious conflict, borders were defined to organize, administer, and defend colonies, and later nations. Being defensible required size, and this often meant amalgamating diverse religious and ethnolinguistic groups. Everywhere the empires introduced diversity, and it mattered little how it was instigated, discrimination followed.

In 1945 when the configuration of the world began changing from empires to nations, national leaders committed to end discrimination by ensuring fundamental freedoms for all. But most did not honor this commitment because discriminatory practices weren't seen as racist, intolerant, elitist, arrogant, sexist, amoral, or illegal. Definitely, not a problem. These were seen as inapplicable western[8] views. Instead, many continued to be charmed by ordered populations; bask in the perpetuation of power, wealth and privilege for select people; and find satisfaction in punishing or 'disciplining" groups deemed troublesome or distasteful. The west would say these practices are products of systemically racist nations. They, however, see it differently. They see it as sensible and natural preferences for majority populations and ordered minority populations. They are sovereign nations. This is their prerogative and comfort zone.

Comfortable or not, western nations became exceptions in embracing the new post-1945 zeitgeist on discrimination; it was immoral and needed to be addressed. These nations had democratic political systems, capitalist-weighted economic systems, and racially white majorities. They became the anti-racist nations. These nations have passed and implemented anti-discrimination legislation, policies, and programs to facilitate level playing fields in their multiracial societies. They present case studies in how complicated discrimination is to address. For these nations it is especially complex because diversity keeps increasing. Many have laid out generous welcome mats for immigrants that vary by race, ethnicity, religion and political views. They offer millions a chance to flee nations where they may face racial, religious, gender, familial or political/thought discrimination, and where corruption, wars or inept governments leave people with little to no hope of experiencing a better life, let alone a level playing field. But increases in diversity instigates an indeterminate increase in *racial* discrimination (see note below). Still, they see it as the right thing to do.

What follows is an overview of the origins and evolution of diversity and discrimination in the Chinese, European, Islamic and Russian empires from 1453-1945. This is followed by a review of racist and anti-racist practices after 1945 for select empire successor states grouped by region. It will become clear that when it comes to discrimination: in most nations, history repeats itself, or nearly so into the 21st century; some nations have outdone history by increasing discrimination; and a minority have broken with history and taken anti-racist paths.

**Note:** Over time, the term racial discrimination has come to refer to discrimination based on race, ethnicity, national origin, or religion. Without additional clarification, this is its usage in this book.

---

Western nations include nations in Western Europe, Australia, Canada, Israel, New Zealand, and the United States. All western nations, but Israel, are successor states to Europe's empires.

# Chinese Empire (pre-1945)

Until the 19th century, the Chinese Empire (221BC – 1912) avoided conflicts with the other competitors for global supremacy. They were content to reign supreme over eastern and most of southeastern Asia. When the empire began declining in the 19th century its realm went on the radar of the European, Japanese and Russian empires. The period 1842–1949 is called China's Century of Humiliation, and there were humiliations aplenty. China had always regarded non-Chinese as inferior – as barbarians. Now the barbarians were besting the Middle Kingdom at every corner and did so for over one hundred years.

Seeing foreigners as barbarians was not unique to China, all of the empires did this. Believing others were uncivilized offered a rationale for conquest—civilizing the barbarians. John Stuart Mill one of the most influential liberal philosophers of the 19th century saw despotism as "a legitimate mode of government in dealing with barbarians, provided the end be in their improvement."[9] The Chinese weren't actually influenced by Mill. They had their own philosophy on barbarians. They didn't want to civilize them; they wanted them to stay away but to acknowledge Chinese superiority through the regular payments of tribute.[10] A Chinese belief in superiority is sacrosanct. Hence the reason the period from 1842 to 1949 is called the Century of Humiliation.

The populations conquered by the Chinese were located in eastern and east-central Asia. They were adjacent Mongoloid ethnolinguistic groups. Uniquely, all conquered people, regardless of their ethnicity and language, were considered Chinese. This did not mean that this was one big happy Chinese family. Discrimination between the ethnically Han Chinese and non-Han Chinese is a theme throughout history, but it remained unaddressed, and it was a source of serious ethnic conflicts.

After the Chinese Empire dissolved, leaders of the Republic of China (1912–1949) knew they had to strengthen defenses against barbarians, but first, they had to end internal ethnic conflict. They started thinking about Chinese ethnicity as denoting a common language and culture, similar to Soviet and western thinking. They oversaw a Sinicization process that required almost all Chinese to adopt the culture and language of the Han. Assimilation was seen as the solution, and compliance was not optional. When the process was complete "ethnicity and nationalization" became "almost interchangeable." [xviii] China transformed diversity into cultural homogeneity. The Han ethnic group became 92% of the population. Being Han was now synonymous with being Chinese.

---

[9] John Stuart Mill also influenced a belief that educated people should be more influential than uneducated. This is a reason some nations restricted the vote to people with educations. He also thought women should be equal. On that point he had zero influence.

[10] The Chinese oversaw a large tributary empire in Asia. To prevent Chinese conquest and to have the privilege of trading with China, nations paid tribute.

The Chinese empire didn't need or want additional labor. Still, every society liked the pliability of slaves to undertake tasks others found objectionable, or even impossible. In China, most slaves were indigenous people. [11] The same was true in its one-time colony Korea, where 1/3rd to ½ of the indigenous population -- the Koreans-- were slaves until the mid-18th century.[i]

Unlike other empires, China's challenge was not insufficient labor but having more labor than it could employ. This created a different discrimination problem. In the 18th and 19th centuries, millions of Chinese became indentured servants and free laborers filling needs for labor in European colonies in Southeast Asia, Africa, and the Americas. One thing was clear to these Overseas Chinese,[12] no one else shared a belief in Chinese superiority.

The Chinese were unique in creating sizeable diasporas all over the world that were unrelated to conquests by the Chinese Empire. They were also unique in not importing foreign labor and in carrying out an obligatory assimilation process that created an ethnolinguistic population that spans one-sixth of the world's population. Having a 92% homogenous population really limits ethnolinguistic discrimination, although this is not evident for the other 8%, many in the 92% that migrate within China for work, and anyone else that is a non-Han resident of China. Discrimination against barbarians has a long and enduring history in China.

## Racism and anti-Racism in Eastern Asia after 1945

(See Appendix for list of countries in Eastern Asia)

Eastern Asian nations have always prized homogeneity. Within this region, China is the most ethnically diverse and the population is 92% Han Chinese.

In 1949, the People's Republic of China (PRC) was created with a Maoist/socialist government. Ethnically homogenous, theoretically classless, and forcing conformance to a common ethos sounded like a formula for eliminating discrimination, but it wasn't. A common ethos turned into another category for discrimination; those with diversity of thought.

During the Cultural Revolution (1966-1976), millions that were educated or had some amount of wealth, which could be something as small as a trinket were imprisoned, tortured, or killed. These were the bourgeoisie, and an obvious enemy and opponent to a classless society. The wealthiest bourgeoisie (200,000 to 2 million) had already been murdered or marginalized in the Chinese Land Reform Movement (1947-1951).[ii] During the Down to the Countryside movement (1968-1975) 17 million "privileged" bourgeoisie urban youth were exiled to the

---

[11] Slavery was abolished in 1910.

[12] Overseas Chinese is a term invented in China to refer to people that do not live in China but were born in China or have Chinese descendants. Living in China, carrying a Chinese passport, or even visiting China are not pre-requisites to being labeled as Overseas Chinese. So deep is the animosity against its one-time conqueror and occupier, Japan, Chinese-Japanese are intentionally excluded from the counts of Overseas Chinese.

countryside, where the only education was farming. These youth became part of the lost generation. Privilege has not been their problem.

It was easy to target "wealthy" opponents. Others were less obvious, but all real or perceived opponents had to be swiftly brought into line. Everyone had to be in agreement with Maoism/socialism for it to work. Diversity of thought had to be extinguished. Under Mao the *laogai,* a reference to China's forced labor camps, also called re-education centers, imprisoned about 10 million annually, most for the crime of opposing Maoism/socialism.[iii,13]

It wasn't just opponents that faced covert, state sanctioned discrimination. The 8% of indigenous people that are non-Han have also faced discrimination. Xinjiang, a Muslim-majority region with a Turkish ethnicity, and Tibet a Buddhist-majority region with a Tibetan ethnicity were annexed by the PRC between 1949 and 1951.[14] These are two of the most populous officially recognized fifty-five minority ethnic groups in China. Both groups have resisted assimilation, both face restrictions on practicing religion and movement, and they are heavily censored. Under the leadership of Mao Zedong about 38 million Muslims, most from Xinjiang, disappeared.[iv] In 2019 about 10% of the Muslim Uighur population of Xinjiang (about 1 million) were in internment camps with allegations of torture, rape, cultural genocide, and brainwashing to purge diversity of thought. The politically correct term for the latter in China is patriotic re-education. Tens of thousands were transferred to factories where there were allegations of forced labor and slavery.[v] The current Dalai Lama said that China has killed 1.2 million Tibetans since the "occupation" began in 1950.[vi] In 2020 an ethnic unity law mandated that all Tibetans undergo Sinicization, or else. Or else what? Tibet is already called the world's largest open-air prison. China argues that foreigners misinterpret the actions it takes against Uighurs and Tibetans. Instead of discriminatory actions they are stern measures directed at separatists. Foreigners undoubtedly misinterpret the stern steps taken against Hong Kongers, too. Hong Kong may soon be called the world's largest open-air prison where inmates learn that expunging diversity of thought is a better option than trying to restore once cherished and protected freedoms.

Tibetans and Muslim Uighurs are two of the fifty-five official minority ethnic groups. An official minority status gives the Chinese government a basis to unequally govern. Both groups have found that unequal can be unwelcome. So have other groups that face discrimination in employment and education. Being an official minority does permit some cultural preservation, but don't tell that to the Tibetans or Uighurs. Permitting cultural preservation could have benefits, like having more than one child when others could not, and drawbacks like prevalent anti-minority behaviors by the Han and other minorities that dislike others receiving preferences. The use of official status for some groups, but not others also creates discriminatory problems for unofficial ethnicities, but the government only wants fifty-five. [vii, viii]

The Chinese also discriminate against many Han Chinese. China's economic expansion relies on migrants from the countryside to work in the cities. These migrants are socially categorized as peasants (*nongmin*). This implies an "inferior

---

[13] The Laogai Museum in Washington DC presents a history of the forced labor camps in China from the 1960s to the present.

[14] Tibet maintains that China's presence is an illegal occupation.

educational and cultural background as well as economic capabilities. The nongmin carry their inferior status with them wherever they migrate." [ix] They are destined to stay inferior because their residential permits (*houkou*) restrict access to many services.[15] In 2015 there were about 278 million nongmin.

Chinese that follow some religions also face discrimination, although some of this may change with a five-year Sinicization of religion program introduced in 2018. All official religions (Buddhism Catholicism, Daoism, Islam and Protestantism) must conform to Chinese government dictates, which means conforming to Chinese socialist thought. If they do, they avoid discrimination. If they don't, there will be persecution. Followers of Judaism, Hinduism and the Falun Gong will not be Sinicized because like all non-official religions they are illegal. Many Falun Gong members are in the laogai, along with many Uighurs. Today the laogai is said to be a collection of more than 1,000 labor camps that has been called "state sponsored slavery."[x]

China is very determined to maintain and even increase homogeneity. Within China they apply pressure to assimilate with "re-education centers," the Ethnic Unity law, and the Sinicization of religion program.

To prevent heterogeneity introduced by foreigners, immigration to China is virtually impossible outside the Special Administrative Regions (SARs) of Hong Kong and Macau. The Chinese are not even accommodating to non-Chinese spouses. They have to regularly renew their visas and pay fees to legally remain in the country. But there is no guarantee that their visas will be renewed and no protections against overt and covert discrimination. In 2020 a sign at McDonalds directed at resident Africans read, "black people are not allowed to enter the restaurant."[xi] Ironically, China doesn't have anti-racism laws. They call racism a western phenomenon.

Korea and China were part of the brief Japanese Empire (1868-1947), and it was not one of racial unity. Nearly 700,000 Koreans were conscripted to work on Japanese farms and factories. As long as Korea was part of the Japanese Empire, they were citizens, conscripted but citizens. After WWII their citizenship was revoked, but they were permitted to stay in Japan. They have faced blatant discrimination, as do other non-Japanese, and mixed-race Japanese. A 2015 article in Newsweek noted that "the racial discrimination that exists in Japan is reminiscent of the segregation-based atmosphere of 1950s America, posing a hostile environment for those of non-Japanese origin."[xii] Non-Japanese are 2.2% of the population. Discrimination for the Korean-Japanese can be exacerbated by their refusal to assimilate into Japanese culture and self-imposing multiculturalism. "It is ethnic identity and the determination to hold onto it that enrages the parties who use hate speech against resident Koreans." The quarter of Korean residents that identify with North Korea, a nation regularly launching missiles into the Sea of Japan, also evokes hate speech.

---

[15] The *houkou* is a residential permit. At birth Chinese people are given access to living areas and different services like schools, universities, and health care. The houkou system is a separate but unequal system. It's overriding purpose is social stability – not equality. The houkou has undergone some changes, but changes must be gradual to maintain social order.

In 2016, Japan passed a toothless hate speech law to comply with a UN Convention on discrimination, but it still does not have laws that forbid discrimination based on race or national origin. Overt discrimination, like racial slurs are common for Koreans and Chinese. The Chinese can also encounter an occasional no Chinese allowed sign. The Chinese (0.5%) are the largest ethnic minority in Japan. Discrimination against them is likely to be seen as *quid pro quo*. School curriculums in China foment discrimination by covering in detail the atrocities perpetrated by the Japanese during WWII. About 80% of Chinese and Japanese have a dim view of each other.[xiii]

Recently South Korea began experimenting with being more receptive to immigrants. Discrimination is in turn increasing. The harsher aspects are directed toward other Asians, including those from the former imperial powers of Japan and China, in addition to Africans. Discrimination against foreigners is probably not as intense in any of these east Asian countries as it is in North Korea. So strong is the desire for a pure race here, if a woman is impregnated by a non-North-Korean there will be no baby. According to a UN commission: "The perpetrators of forced abortions and infanticide appear to be driven by an official ideology that emphasizes the importance of maintaining the purity of the Korean race at all costs."[xiv]

Japan, South Korea, and China are on trajectories for significant population declines in the 21st century. One solution could be immigration, but the obstacles to lessening homogeneity are legal and social, and this creates real challenges. In Japan and South Korea national leaders know that immigration offers a solution to their declining populations. S. Korea has made a little progress, but both struggle to get legislators and voters to agree to new policies that will lessen homogeneity. Everyone knows that increased diversity will lead to increased discrimination. All they have to do is look to the Americas, Europe, or Australia.

Autocratic China doesn't have to be concerned with getting buy in from the masses to change its immigration policy. The government can do what it wants. In 2020 it displayed some latitude to allow highly-skilled foreigners with the carrot of a permanent 10-year resident card – not naturalized citizenship. The masses can't change what the government does, but sometimes they are permitted to comment on government policies without repercussions. Responses on social media were blatantly racist. Once called barbarians, foreigners are commonly referred to as foreign trash. The most degrading and disturbing comments were for black foreigners. They echoed comments made by the Ku Klux Clan 150 years ago in America.[xv] The great Chinese firewall censors anything and everything it does not want the Chinese to discuss or foreigners to see. It may be that impugning foreigners, including highly skilled permanent residents, is consistent with promoting Chinese superiority.

Nations in Eastern Asia are among the world's most homogenous populations. Per western definitions, they are also among the most racist societies on earth. These nations generally do not see their highly selective immigration policies, forced assimilation, racist slights and slurs, and legal or condoned unequal treatment as a big problem in need of addressing. Most of their citizens may not even see them as racist, or discriminatory. They too, may believe that these are western views. These are eastern nations that see great benefits to preserving order and cultural homogeneity, especially when compared to the challenges that western nations face with their diverse and obviously disordered populations.

## Islamic empires (pre-1945)

A long history of Christians and Muslims fighting over religious followers inspired the competition for global supremacy. The final straw was delivered in 1453 when the Ottoman Empire/Turkish Empire (1299–1922),[16] finished off the first Christian empire, Byzantium (330–1453).[17] For the next 150 years, the Ottoman Empire sowed fear throughout Christendom, also called Europe.

Religion was always center stage in the Islamic empires. With the conquest of new lands and people, religion was a key determinant to social order. Religionism was the primary form of racism. Muslims sat atop the social hierarchy. Actually, not all Muslims. Sectarianism between Catholics and Protestants endured in Europe for 100 years in the 16th and 17th centuries, but sectarianism between Sunnis and Shias is as old as Islam. In the Sunni Ottoman Empire, Sunnis were trusted and on top and Shias were untrusted and on the bottom.

Below the trusted Sunnis were the *dhimmis*. Dhimmis were select groups, mostly Christians and Jews, that enjoyed a somewhat protected status and were permitted to practice religion in designated millets.[18] Millets are an early implementation of multiculturalism based on religion. (The idea behind multiculturalism is to allow different populations to live in separate communities where they are given freedom to maintain their cultures. The millets permitted maintaining religious cultures. They operated as separate but unequal communities.) Millets have been extolled as symbolic of religious tolerance in the Ottoman Empire. Tolerance had limits. Dhimmis were a subordinated class, they paid burdensome taxes, endured public humiliation, and were easily identified by prescribed clothing and markings on their homes.[19] Compared to Christians that were enslaved in the empire, living in a Christian millet was clearly more tolerant. There was even more tolerance for trusted Christians. This included Christian sex slaves in the harems, those serving as administrators in the government, and members of the Janissary Corp., an elite infantry unit that served the sultan.

Below the dhimmis were Muslims categorized as heretics, such as Shias, in addition to slaves. The worst discrimination was directed at the Shias. One Ottoman sultan, Selim I (1512–1520) said, "the killing of one Shia had as much otherworldly reward as killing seventy Christians."

---

[6] The Ottoman Empire was the largest, most powerful, and durable Islamic empire. It might have existed longer if it had not been a principal ally with the Central Powers in WWI. The losing empires had to disband their empires after the war.

[7] It was also called the Eastern Roman Empire. It was the last remnant of the Roman Empire.

[8] Millets contained groupings of people of like religions that were permitted to apply their own religious laws. Millets still had to adhere to applicable Ottoman laws.

[9] The humiliating practice of forcing people to display identifiable marks was not limited to the Ottomans. In the Era of Empire, for example, Jews and Muslims in the Spanish Inquisition, Jews in the Safavid Empire, and Jews in Nazi Germany were required to do something similar.

Ottoman intolerance increased in the late 19th and early 20th centuries. Between 1894 and 1917 more than a million Christian Armenians were massacred. [20] Massacres were also inflicted on Christian Bulgarians (1913), Christian Assyrians (1914–1923), Christian Greeks (1914–1923), and Kurdish-speaking Yazidis.[21] Early on these massacres coincided with a decision to make Christians equal to Muslims. American law professor Mark Movsesian has tied these massacres to the rejection of Christian equality. He said, "law that does not reflect the values of a society is bound to fail." Further, "if the conflict between the law and values is great, and touches a society's core beliefs, significant disorder, including violence against vulnerable communities, can easily occur."[vii]

Beginning in 1913, the massacres bore the imprimatur of the Young Turks. Endeavoring to create a homogenous Turkish-speaking Sunni Muslim state in Anatolia (Turkey), they saw religious diversity as a problem in need of a solution. Their behaviors and motives have been compared to Hitler in his quest for a pure Aryan nation. In total, an estimated 3.5 million Christians were eliminated or about 80% of the empire's total, and 20% of the population of Turkey. The Young Turks did come close to achieving their slogan "Turkey for the Turks."[xvi]

The Islamic Mughal Empire was centered on the Indian sub-continent. Tolerance is not a hotly contested topic because, excepting some enlightened rulers, this empire displayed a rare level of intolerance for the beliefs and followers of Hinduism and Buddhism. Both were considered polytheistic faiths,[22] and in Islam, polytheists are guilty of Islam's most serious sin, shirk. Many Hindus and Buddhists underwent forced conversions, while others fled or tried too. Estimates for murdered Hindus range from 60 to 400 million.[xvii] This episode of violence is commonly referred to as the Hindu Holocaust, "but it was rationalized by the Islamic conquerors as a "religious duty to smite non-believers."[v,xviii] By the 19th century Hinduism had been virtually extinguished outside Bali, Indonesia and the Indian subcontinent.

"The Islamic conquest of India is probably the bloodiest story in history. It is a discouraging tale, for its evident moral is that civilization is a precious good, whose delicate complex of order and freedom, culture and peace, can at any moment be overthrown by barbarians invading from without or multiplying within."[xix]

In 1501 the Ottomans outlawed Shiite Islam in the lands of the Persian Safavids. This motivated Shah Ismail to build a Shiite empire to challenge the Ottomans. In the Safavid Empire Twelver Shias and only Twelver Shias could practice their faith in peace. In 1501 Persia's population was mostly Sunni. Each non-Jew had the option of voluntarily or forcibly converting to Twelver Shiism or death. Persian Jews were permitted to live as a ritually unclean race. Shah Ismail was not the first or last to force assimilation, cleanse non-assimilators, eliminate diversity of thought, and marginalize select populations to eliminate conflict and strengthen the hand of government.

---

[20] The 1915-1917 massacre of Armenians is recognized by some as the Armenian Genocide. Turkey considers the cleansing of Armenians and other populations horrible but not premeditated genocide.

[21] The Yazidis are Kurdish people that practice a unique syncretic blend of Christianity, Islam, and Zoroastrianism.

[22] Buddhism is not a polytheistic faith because it has no gods, but because there is a belief in many devas which some describe as god-like, it is sometimes inaccurately categorized as polytheistic.

Something similar occurred when building the first Saudi state (1744-1818). The Saudi state's two founders Mohammed bin Saud, and religious leader Abd al-Wahhab thought the adoption of western practices like European music and painting, were heretical to Islam and responsible for the Ottoman Empire's declining state. The founders were on a mission to purify Sunni Islam. Apostates, heretics, and infidels (mostly Christians and Jews) were out. The idolatry practicing Shiite and Sufi Muslims were considered heretical and their practices not even Islamic. Like other non-Muslims, they converted, were isolated, forcibly expelled, or killed.[xx]

Religionism was the primary form of racism, but race-based discrimination was not insignificant and most evident in the Arab slave trade. Between the 7th and 20th centuries millions of non-Muslims were forcibly removed from their homelands during the Arab slave trade. "Wars of religion," which could be a pretext for acquiring slaves, could be waged in order to capture and enslave non-Muslims. It was illegal for Muslims to enslave Muslims. Various estimates made from minimal records[23] place the number enslaved during this trade at 20–200 million with 10–20 million sold, and 10–190 million dying before being sold.[xxi,24] Two common causes of death were castration and infanticide. Castration was common for black slaves,[25] and only 1 in 6 to 10 survived.[xxii] The rationales for castration were to limit temptation and procreation.[xxiii] Infanticide was a near certainty for the babies of black female slaves serving as concubines or sex slaves for their lighter skinned Muslim owners.[xxiv] Murdering mulatto infants were "a mere matter of course, and without the least remorse or dread."[xxv]

Most slaves were black Africans, but some were east and central Asian, Turkish, Persian, and European. What they shared in common was they were non-Muslim. Slaves sold in the Ottoman Empire between the 14th and 19th centuries were 15–40% European.[26] Enslaved for their faith these are the "faith slaves." This period coincides with Ottoman conquests in the Balkans in the 14th to 16th centuries when there was mass enslavement of Christians.[xxvi,27] Similarly, it coincides with the presence of the Crimean Khanate in Eastern Europe. This was as a vassal state of the Ottoman Empire between 1449 and 1783. This khanate was a slave *entrepôt* that supplied an estimated 2 million white Christian Russian, Polish, and Lithuanians slaves. Another 1-1.25 million Christians, mostly from Italy, Spain, and Portugal were enslaved, sold or ransomed by Ottoman/Barbary pirates in the 18th and 19th centuries.[xxvii] "Some people assume that faith slavery, because it was not race based, was less brutal or dehumanizing. Nothing could be further from the truth." "Just as with black Africans, faith slaves were considered commodities to be bought and

---

[23] Senegalese author Tidiane N'Diaye explained a reason for the paucity of data. "Most of the African authors have not yet published a book on the Arab-Muslim slave trade out of religious solidarity. There are 500 million Muslims in Africa, and it is better to blame the West than talk about the past crimes of Arab Muslims."

[24] This includes the children of female slaves automatically killed at birth.

[25] Castration was much more common for black slaves because white slaves had greater    protections, like Christian polities prohibiting castration. Some Christians were said to be castrated in Muslim Spain (800-1492).

[26] Christian polities prohibiting castration gave white slaves a far greater chance of making it to the slave markets. This made the numbers for enslaved and sold much closer for whites than blacks.

[27] Some Christian slave traders in Venice and Genoa sold Christian slaves in the Ottoman Empire.

sold. If anything, religious intolerance justified extremely cruel and harsh treatment."[xxviii]

The Arab slave trade gained extra vigor in the 19th century when European empires outlawed the trade in slaves. Zanzibar (today part of Tanzania), a 19th-century slave entrepôt ruled by Omani Arabs worked with African chiefs to fill requests.[xxix, xxx, xxxi,28,29]

The Arab slave trade endured much longer and processed more slaves than the Atlantic slave trade, but little tangible evidence was left behind in the primary market, the Middle East. Surviving European Christian slaves returned to Europe when manumitted or otherwise freed. For black slaves, the combination of castration, infanticide and encouraging manumitted slaves to return to Africa limited any enduring presence beyond some mixed-race descendants that managed to survive.

All of the major Islamic empires had long-lasting impacts on discriminatory practices in their successor states in MENA and South Asia. Chief among them is intra-faith, inter-faith, and racial discrimination.

## Racism in the Middle East and North Africa after 1945
(See Appendix for list of countries)

The Middle East and North African (MENA) region comprises much of the area ruled by the Ottoman Empire. Most nations in this region became independent in the mid-20th century. Independence followed the dissolution of the Ottoman Empire and a period of 4 to 52 years of oversight by the infidel Christian British or French. As signatories to the UN Charter each nation committed to equal fundamental freedoms for all, but as independent sovereigns, this commitment was based on the honor system. Each nation had the power to end, modify or perpetuate discriminatory practices. All of the above occurred with extra weighting on modification and perpetuation.

The Ottoman millet system showed some tolerance for Christians and Jews as subordinated populations. To become independent, national leaders had to agree to end the subordination of Jews and Christians. The response was unofficial subordination. The intolerance for the mostly indigenous Jews and Christians grew quickly. Discriminatory practices included asset confiscations, expulsions, pogroms,[30] inability to openly worship, and terrorism. They were sending an unambiguous message, if they couldn't subordinate/discriminate against Christians and Jews they would make emigrating the best option. In 1910 Christians made up 14% of the Middle East's population, in 2016 it was 4%.[xxxii] Between 1910 and 1919, countries

---

[28] Traders in the Arab slave trade involved not only Arabs and Africans but also Persians, Turkish and Indians. Trading in people was considered another way for people to make money and a particularly lucrative one.

[29] While visiting the Omani National Museum of History in 2018 I found a painting of Omani Arabs working in their colony in Zanzibar. I told my guide this was a slave entrepôt. He said, slavery is not part of Omani history. Apparently, it's been cancelled.

[30] Pogroms are violent riots with a goal to expel or murder targeted populations.

in MENA measured their Jewish populations with four, five, or six digits.[xxxiii] In 2016, Jews in MENA countries, outside Israel, were commonly counted with three or fewer digits.

Christians and Jews similarly vacated North African nations when they became independent. The Christians were mostly European transplants that had arrived during Europe's colonial period (1830-1968).[31] Many Jews had arrived in the 15th and 16th centuries during the Spanish Inquisition, but some were indigenous. Shortly after the Suez Crisis (1956),[32] Egypt's President Nasser oversaw the expulsion of Europeans and resident Jews. In 1970, Libya's Muammar Gaddafi oversaw the expulsion of Italians (Catholics) and the confiscation of their assets. Jews were also expelled.[xxxiv] Shortly after Algerian independence in 1962, there was an exodus of around 900,000 *pied noirs*.[33]

European Christians also vacated the Sudan, but not the indigenous Christians. The south had a majority indigenous Christian population. The north had a majority Muslim and a minority Christian population. Christians in the north and south remained in an unhappy co-existence with their fellow Muslim nationals. A history of slavery was fundamental to fractured relations. Beginning in the 19th century, Sudan's role in the Arab slave trade was vigorous. Southern Christian Sudanese were enslaved by northern Arab Muslim Sudanese and sold to buyers in Egypt and the Ottoman Empire.[xxxv] An estimated 2/3rds of the residents of Khartoum were slaves in this period. This coincides with the approximate size of the black population. The trade *legally* continued until 1924,[xxxvi] even though Sudan had become part of the British Empire in 1899 where slavery had been illegal since 1834.

In an independent Sudan (1956), northern Muslims and southern Christians experienced thirty-nine years of north-south civil wars. In 1988 conquered Christians were being sold for between $30 and $80. Conquered non-Muslims were still being enslaved in 2005. [xxxvii, xxxviii]

Discrimination in the Sudan was and is not limited to Christians; it has extended to Muslims, and people with darker skin. This may seem odd because outside the South the Sudanese population is overwhelmingly darker-skinned Muslims. It seems that brown, which is associated with Arabs, is better than black, which is associated with Africans. Who is Arab and who is African has been a central driver of discrimination in the Sudan. Some tribes self-identify as Arab or African based on language, profession, or choice. Because Arabs have had the most political and religious power and privilege, many tribes self-identified as Arab. This became a problem. During the War in Darfur (2003-present) the Sudanese government endeavored to homogenize the population by cleansing it of African Muslims, and anyone else whose self-categorization as Arab they rejected.[xxxix] In 2003, "Arabs" ~~murdered 70,000 black Africans~~. Enslavement of Africans was practiced in this war,

[31] Algeria was colonized by the French in 1830. Others in North Africa weren't colonized by European empires for at least another 60 years.

[32] In 1956 Egyptian President Nassar nationalized the Suez Canal. Israel, Britain and France unsuccessfully launched military operations to retake the canal. Per treaty, the Canal was supposed to stay under British management until 1968. This failed operation is attributed to a lack of support from the US, Soviet Union, and the UN. This failure is seen as symbolic of the end of empire.

[33] Pied noirs were Christians and Jews of mostly Spanish, Italian, Maltese, French, and Palestinian origins or descent.

too. The International Criminal Court investigated allegations of genocide, war crimes, and crimes against humanity. Sudanese President Al-Bashir became the first sitting president wanted by the International Criminal Court (ICC). This did not deter the African Dignity Forum from honoring him in 2016 as an outstanding African leader.[xl,xli] In 2020 black Sudanese are still referred to in the media and routinely called slaves, negroes and monkeys.

Forced emigration and marginalization didn't end the disdain felt for Christians in the region. Four infidel Christian powers (Britain, France, Italy, and the United States) had defeated the Ottomans in WWI leaving Islam without a seat on the global stage and without a caliphate to unite Muslims. Leaders of Muslim fundamentalist groups oozed anti-western and anti-Christian venom. Beginning in 1998 some devastating terrorist attacks were executed on western nations. In the 21st century Islamic militants were attempting to reclaim lands lost to the Christian empires since the 15th century and reinforcing the dhimmi system on "conquered" Christians. Islamic militancy was supported by millions of Muslims across the globe. To many others, this was racism in one of its evilest forms. [xlii,xliii]

MENA's population appears relatively homogenous from the perspectives of language and religion. It would be easy to erroneously assume that being relatively homogenous would limit discrimination. Any differences in religion or language drive discrimination. All nations in MENA are Arabic speaking with the exception of Iran (Persian-speaking), Israel (Hebrew-speaking), and Turkey (Turkish-speaking). People that speak Arabic, speak the same language of Islamic sacred texts and the Prophet Muhammad, while the others do not. Islam sees all Muslims as equal, but perceptions of superiority for people that speak Arabic are prevalent.

This region counts among the most religiously homogenous.[34] Ironically it is also the region with the greatest amount of religious discrimination and conflict. With the exception of Israel, all are Muslim nations. However, sectarianism between Sunnis and Shias has instigated wars since the 7th century and continues to do so. Cross intra-Muslim conflict and discrimination did subside in the early 1800s, but it began rising in 1979 with the election of Iran's Shiite Supreme Leader, Ayatollah Khomeini. He was on a mission to unify Muslims under his rule. There was one exception: Muslims with diversity of thought. In 1988 he issued a fatwa that called for the murder of Muslims in Iran who disagreed with his positions. Thirty thousand were executed.[xliv]

Khomeini's unifying mission was not persuasive to the rulers of Sunni-majority nations. Forty-four out of forty-nine Muslim-majority nations have Sunni majorities. Among these forty-four is Saudi Arabia, the de facto leader of the Muslim world. Instead, his mission brought to the foreground a fundamentalist Sunni belief that the Shias are heretical Muslims.[xxiii] In 2017, one of Saudi Arabia's most highly regarded religious scholars said of the Shias, "they are not our brothers ... rather they are brothers of Satan ..."[xlv]

---

[34] Homogeneity with respect to being Arabic speaking and Sunni Muslim is facilitated by making it near impossible for foreigners to become naturalized citizens. This is especially true on the Arabian Peninsula. In 2019, Saudi Arabia announced some flexibility to encourage scientists and doctors to immigrate.

Khomeini failed in his mission to unite and rule the Muslim community. Instead, he reignited and exacerbated sectarian conflict that is clearly manifested in the never-nding Shiite Iran - Sunni Saudi proxy wars. This conflict has led to many deadly errorist acts in western nations, and the regular terrorizing of Muslims in many of he forty-nine Muslim majority nations. These proxy wars include the Yemeni Civil War (2015–?), the Syrian Civil War (2011–?), and Iraqi Civil War (2014–2017). In he latter, the murder of Shias, in addition to Yazidis and Christians has been haracterized as genocides.[xlvi] Khomeini also supercharged hatred of Jewish Israel in he global Muslim community.

The Mandate for Palestine allocated land for a future Jewish nation in the MENA egion. The Ottomans had conquered this land from the Jews in the 16th century, but n the early 20th century the Ottomans were conquered. The mandate was created vith unanimous support from the League of Nations fifty-one members. At this time, here were no Arab members in the League because there were no independent Arab ations. Opposition from Arab populations was forceful, and continuous. Later, the Jnited Nations (successor to the League of Nations) modified the mandate to artition it into future Arab and Jewish states, but this had little impact on Arab eceptivity. On May 14, 1948 Israel became an independent sovereign. On May 15, 948, the first of many Arab-Israeli wars commenced. In spite of aspects of religious, istorical, and linguistic homogeneity, this region has lacked unity with one xception; their desire to eject a Zionist/Jewish state from the region.

Surrounded by Arab nations seeking its demise, Israel needed the UN to validate ts sovereignty and deter Muslim nations from violating it. This did not occur. Even fter the Holocaust, sympathy for the Jews was hardly universal, and it took a turn or the worse when the Arabs lost the 1967 Arab-Israeli War and Israel began ccupying lands designated for a future Palestinian state. Most developing nations[35] n the UN General Assembly were anti-Semitic or anti-Zionist. In 1975 the UN jeneral Assembly passed resolution 3379 declaring Zionism as a form racism. There vere 72 votes for, 35 against and 32 abstentions. Contrary to its Charter to protect he sovereignty of member nations, the United Nations was effectively denying the ight of one of its sovereign members to exist. The resolution was revoked sixteen ears later in 1991.

Ongoing discrimination against Jews around the world rarely garners attention utside Israel. The nation of Israel is considered in the same breath with North Korea nd Iran.[xlvii] Instead, the Jews are more likely to be cast as imperial racists denying Palestinians statehood. The general view is that it is the Palestinians that face iscrimination. No question Israel's occupation of lands allocated for a Palestinian tate since the 1967 Arab-Israeli War subjugates the Palestinians, but from an Israeli erspective it is also necessary until both parties agree to peace. Having a belligerent hat is supported by people and nations all over the world poses an existential threat, nd Israel can hardly rely on the UN, per its' Charter, to protect its' sovereignty.

Israel has survived the repeated attempts to end its existence. The global Jewish opulation in 1933 was about 15 million. This was also its population in 2018. oday, the Jews live relatively free of religious persecution within Israel, but they

---

[5] Developed nations have advanced and stable institutions, and their people enjoy very high qualities of ife. Developing nations have none of the above.

live with anti-Semitism or anti-Zionism around the globe. Twenty-nine nations deny Israel's UN status as a sovereign,[36] and fifteen deny Israelis the right to enter their countries.

There is no fundamental freedom of religion in this region and religionism is the greatest generator of discrimination. But it is not the only basis for discrimination, racial discrimination is also salient. With encouragement from JFK, the Arab slave trade ended in 1962, when Saudi Arabia officially ended the trade.[37] Still there are very few black citizens in this region. A commonly used term for a black person in Arabic is abd; it means slave. A trade in dark-skinned people, catering to Arabs on the Arabian Peninsula has continued through online slave markets that leverage Instagram and other online applications. [xlviii] In 2017 open air slave markets in Libya were reported. The enslaved were black Africans trying to migrate to Europe. The enslavers and buyers were lighter skinned Arabs. In 1981, North Africa's Mauritania became the last nation in the world to abolish slavery, but 10-20% are still enslaved. [xlix] Many inherited their status. Slaves are mostly black, and their masters lighter skinned "Arabs."

The other large group that faces severe discrimination, outside women, are migrant laborers, also called guest workers. In several nations on the Arabian Peninsula, migrant workers are more numerous than citizens. Most are Muslims from India, Pakistan, Bangladesh, and the Philippines. Some also come from Egypt and some nations in northeast sub-Saharan Africa. Most people have dark skin, and those with lighter skin get higher paying jobs. There are many slave-like stories about the lives of migrant workers. Sexual abuse of female workers is regularly documented. Those that have it better have stories that sound more like indentured servants, or untouchables that *inter alia* (among other things) endure exploitative working conditions and close living quarters. In some cities they are directed to separate public washrooms. Still, millions apply to work here to support their families back home.

Note: South Asia is another region that was ruled by an Islamic empire – the Mughal Empire. Post-1945 diversity and discrimination is covered under the European empires because their rule followed Islamic rule.

---

[36] Unanimous recognition of sovereignty is the rule with few exceptions. Four nations have one hold out, and China has fourteen that continue to recognize Taiwan as the legitimate government of China.

[37] Slavery was not legally abolished in the Middle East until 1970 (Oman) and in North Africa, 1981 (Mauritania).

# The Russian Empire (1721-1917)

The Russian sphere of influence must be treated differently from the perspective of discrimination pre-and post-1945 because there was no clean break in 1945. The Russian Empire dissolved in 1917 and was replaced with the Soviet Union (1922-1991). That's not the reason for the unclean break. The Soviet Union was an original signatory to the UN Charter in 1945. They committed to ending the subordination of colonial/territorial populations, and to deliver equal fundamental freedoms to all. The reason is that it did neither. After WWII, nations in the Soviet Union did not have the possibility of becoming independent, and satellite nations from Central Europe were added to the Soviet sphere.[38] Most were added involuntarily. When it came to fundamental freedoms for all, there were fundamental freedoms for none. After 1991, the nature of discrimination changed again, although some historical resemblances were uncanny. This is why there are three distinct periods for the Russian sphere: 1721-1917 (Russian Empire), 1922-1991 (Soviet Union), and post-1991 (Russia).

**The Russian Empire** (1721-1917) was last to enter the competition for global supremacy. Much of its expansion came from conquering lands from the Ottoman and Safavid empires. The empires were in decline, making them easy targets. They were also desirable targets. The Russian Empire was an Eastern Orthodox Catholic empire that sometimes fancied itself as the Third Rome. The Second Rome was the Byzantine Empire. It had been conquered by the Muslim Ottomans, who then subjugated about 8 million followers of Eastern Orthodoxy and enslaved 2 million white Christian (many Eastern Orthodox) Russian, Polish, and Lithuanians. There was a score or two to settle.

The Russians built their empire by conquering contiguous lands in Asia and Europe. People were white,[39] and ethnolinguistically Slavic, Turkic, Persian, European and Inorodtsy. The latter was an "other" Russian category. Religious diversity was primarily Christian, Islamic and Jewish. Within these diverse populations, discrimination fell hardest on Muslims and Jews. When the Russians annexed the Crimean Khanate in 1783, Muslims were strongly encouraged to relocate to the Ottoman Empire. In the 19th century, the empire annexed much of Central Asia, in addition to Chechnya, Ingushetia, Dagestan, and Circassia in the Caucasus. To help manage Muslim populations in Central Asian colonies, Russians were transported in. The solution for managing Muslim populations in the Caucasus, which became part of Russia proper, was religious cleansing. An estimated 90% were cleansed primarily through forced deportations to Iran, Turkey, and Siberia. Many died *en route*.[1]

The empire acquired a large Jewish population when parts of Poland were annexed in the late 18th century. In 1804, legislation was passed that restricted the movement and employment of Jews. Later in the century, things worsened for the

---

[38] The Soviet sphere consisted of the fifteen republics of the Soviet Union, and the nations in Central Europe except Yugoslavia after 1948 and Albania after 1961. (Central Europe was called Eastern Europe when it was part of the Soviet sphere.)

[39] People from Central Asia are commonly of Turkic and Persian descent, and they are considered white rather than Asian. This may be an American standard and not universal.

Jews. The empire was undergoing a Russian nationalization campaign, and the Jews didn't fit the model.[li] Between 1881 and 1914 more than 2 million Jews left Russia, and 1.75 million went to the United States.[lii]

There was an even larger group that faced discrimination in this empire. Half of the indigenous population were serfs. When slavery was abolished in 1723, serfdom began. The owners of the slaves/serfs saw this as a change of nomenclature. The empire began declining in the mid 19th century. Fearing the possibility of half the population revolting; the serfs were freed in 1861.

## Racism and anti-Racism in the Soviet Union (1922-1991)

In the Soviet Union increasing diversity did not inevitably result in increasing discrimination. The Soviet Union had a communist/socialist[40] political and economic system with an underlying premise of comrades in a classless society with social and economic equality. Theoretically, this dispenses with many bases for discrimination. There was also an internationalization policy that mandated ethnic bonhomie, a religious policy that everyone was atheist, and people were racially white. People with diverse ethnicities and religions were homogenized by fiat. This theoretically dispensed with many other bases for discrimination.

There was, however, heterogeneity of thought and this had to end. Like Chinese Socialism, fundamental freedoms, like freedom of speech and religion, were anathema to Soviet Socialism. [41] In order for Soviet Socialism to work, everyone had to be singing from the same hymnal page. Anyone on a different page became the grandest basis for discrimination. Opponents included people of religion who opposed atheism, "wealthy" people fighting the confiscation of their land and other assets, advocates of personal freedoms resisting repression, anyone that was perceived to have diverse political views, and anyone that could not be trusted as a Soviet socialist. The heavy lifting of delivering homogeneity of thought was carried out by Premier Joseph Stalin (1922–1952). Up to 18 million opponents of various ethnicities, were transported into the Soviet camps and colonies of the gulag labor system.[liii]About 2-3 million died. [liv]

The absence of a fundamental freedom from arbitrary actions of the state affected millions. Between 1935 and 1949 relocation initiatives transported large populations of untrusted Crimean, Finnish, Romanian, Estonian, Latvian, Lithuanian, Polish, and Ukrainians nearer to trusted Russians. Ukrainians weren't just transported, millions were starved. In the *Holodomor* (1932–1933) an estimated four million Ukrainians starved to death in a Soviet instigated human-made famine that aimed to end even murmurs of dissent.[lv,lvi] Several nations have categorized the Holodomor as genocide. To Stalin it was simply ensuring success of Soviet Socialism. One of Stalin's favorite expressions was "a person, a problem, no person—no problem."[lvii] (In 2017 the Russians voted Stalin the most outstanding person in world history.)

---

[40] There is little agreement on the differences between socialism and communism, and many use the terms interchangeably. Both are supposed to have a foundation of social and economic equality.

[41] The Soviets used a brand of socialism called Marxism-Leninism. The particular brand of socialism used by Stalin is called Stalinism.

The untrusted populations above were Christian, or former Christians when atheism became the official religion. There were also many untrusted non-Christian populations. In 1943 and 1944 Stalin oversaw the transport of Turkic Muslims from Crimea and Chechnya to Soviet republics in Central Asia.[lviii] "The entire Karachi population, Kalmyks, Chechen and Ingush peoples, Balkars, Crimean Tatars and Meskhetian Turks were rounded up and expelled; those who could not be moved were shot, their villages burned to the ground."[lix] Muslims were being punished for allegedly collaborating with the Nazis, an accusation that holds little credibility outside Russia. Nearly 200,000 Muslims or virtually the area's entire Muslim population were transported. This transport is categorized as ethnic cleansing,[lx] or in the case of the Council of Europe, genocide because so many died in the process.

After WWII, Jewish hatred in the Soviet sphere remained high. In 1948 it worsened. Stalin saw Soviet Jews as a fifth column, and they suffered severe repression and purges. Then he forbade Jews from leaving. Racist violence against Jews skyrocketed in the 1980s. [lxi] This is when restrictions were removed, and an estimated 1.6 million Russian Jews and their relatives emigrated. Israel and the United States remained favored destinations, but Germany had also become accessible and welcoming.

British historian Norman Davies estimated that 50 million in the Soviet sphere died of *unnatural non-wartime* causes between 1925 and 1953. Other estimates range from 20–100 million.

What about social equality for the classless trusted populations? There were actually two social classes: Communist Party members and the masses. Party members held power, and this enabled the accumulation of wealth and privilege that was forbidden to the masses. In a so-called classless society, this was a source of suffering in silence. Police ubiquity ensured voices were repressed. The masses were anyway unhappy with their flatter less discriminating hierarchy because social equality implied being poor with no opportunity for change. This reality eventually led to the dissolution of the Soviet Union in 1991, the end of the Cold War in 1991, and the acknowledgement that socialism was not superior to democratic capitalism.

## Racism and anti-Racism in Russia after 1991

The dissolution of the Soviet Union in 1991 led to the arrival of twenty-eight independent nations from the regions of Eastern Europe, Central Asia, and Central Europe. When this occurred, discrimination soared. Without being forced to get along and practice atheism, overt ethnic and religious discrimination rose significantly. Within Russia, the re-ascendancy of Russian Orthodoxy led to a revival in discrimination against Muslims and Jews. Discrimination against Muslims has been exacerbated by separatist movements and terrorism.

Russia is often compared to the United States as a land of immigrants, but Russia's immigrants are mostly migrant workers (temporary laborers) from adjoining former Soviet republics. Most are Muslims from Central Asia that live in migrant camps in Russia. During Soviet times Central Asia's Muslims were comrades. As non-Soviet migrant laborers they have faced harsh discrimination, including violence, wage theft, and harsh exploitation.[lxii] "Racist violence now occurs on an almost daily basis." Muslims are one target and Roma are another. Generally, anyone non-Slavic is a target of discrimination. This includes non-Slavic Russians.[lxiii] Much of this is illegal but seeking enforcement from police can make things worse.[lxiv] Police are known to be extremely biased against non-Slavic Russians and to arbitrarily engage in inhumane practices."[lxv] Russian law enforcement agencies even promote race-based inhumanity by legally hosting paramilitary training for racist groups from all over the world.[lxvi]

Russia, like the Soviet Union, also discriminates against people with diverse political views. Diverse views are repressed by state control of the media. For those that succeed in communicating opposing and critical views of the government, the government leverages intimidation, imprisonment and assassinations.

Black populations in Russia are less than a percent, and little is known about discrimination beyond anecdotes, like fans making monkey noises at black footballers, numerous incidents, including one by a Russian legislator, that portrayed American President Obama as a monkey, and African university students finding racist insults, including being called a monkey, so common they ignore them. It's not just African students that experience racism, Asian students, really any non-Slavic Russian students have been victims of violence.[lxvii]

A survey in Russia and twenty-eight other European states in 2019 asked respondents if their country would be better with more immigrants. On an 11-point scale, where 0 was a worse place to live, Russia's average response was 3.3. Among the two lowest. In other studies, 78% of Russians were found to have a negative view of immigrants and 53% would support a permanent ban on immigrants.[lxviii]

Groups that face discrimination in Russia include immigrants, non-Slavic Russian citizens, migrants, non-Christians, homosexuals, and women.[42] Excluding women, this is up to 40% of the people residing in Russia. It's Russia for the straight, Christian, ethnic Russians – but only men. Racism in Russia is pervasive, but instead of being seen as a problem, it is seen as reinforcing superior Russian values. [lxix]

# Intra-European empires (pre-1945)

In Europe, the competition for empire took two distinct paths: some competitors focused on building intra-European empires, and some overseas colonial empires. In either case, ruling Europe was considered essential to global supremacy, and this made the competition within Europe particularly intense. Continuous wars are part of Europe's history. Continuous wars portended continuous changes to diversity and discrimination. Borders often changed and this meant regularly amalgamating and dividing different ethnic populations. Wars and aftermaths also led to voluntary or forcible population shifts, ethnic cleansings, and genocides.

Before the Islamic conquest of Iberia in the 8th century, Europe had a homogenous population that was white and Christian with a small Jewish population.

---

[42] In 2020 same sex marriage was banned. In 2017 violence against women was decriminalized unless they require treatment in a hospital.

When Spain and Portugal (Iberia) had Muslim rule (900-1478), dark- and light-skinned Muslims were added to the mix. This was a period when Muslims and Jews were superior to Christians and enslavers and traders in Christians.[lxx] During the Spanish Inquisition (1478–1834) policies were implemented to restore blood purity to Iberia. The goal of the Inquisition was to convert or cleanse Muslims and Jews. Many converted,[43] many were killed, and about 460,000 Muslims and Jews migrated to different locations, including the Polish Lithuanian Commonwealth and the Ottoman Empire.[lxxi,44] The Spanish Inquisition was not the last example of erasing religious diversity in Europe. For centuries, religionism was the primary form of racism in an ethnically diverse but almost exclusively white Europe.

Religious discrimination in Europe was not all inter-faith; it was also intra-Christian. The 16th and 17th centuries were plagued by wars between the Roman Catholics and the Protestants.[45] At the end of the wars, there was a sign of acceptance of Christian diversity between states, but not within them. A state, for example, would be all Catholic or all Lutheran. Having in-state religious homogeneity was important to ending conflict and discrimination. Many following unofficial Christian faiths fled to the Thirteen Colonies, but most, remained and faced discrimination. Among the most discriminated were Britain's Irish Catholics. It took until 1829 for Catholic Emancipation to be considered complete. Even then, the generally poor Irish Catholics remained subordinated to wealthier Protestant British landowners.

European states were no different from other states in the world; they preferred populations to be homogenous. It was in Europe where the notion of a sovereign nation-state having a homogenous population was born. Homogeneity implied ethnic and religious uniformity.[46] White was taken for granted. With the designation of official religions, Europe's early nation states were white and religiously uniform. Ethnicity varied, but this was homogenized through a process of assimilation into common nationalities.

Europe had a long history of slavery. Slaves were white and non-Christian. This was followed by a few centuries where up to 75% of the population were serfs. By the 16th century, Europe was moving away from forms of involuntary servitude. This was less so in the south. In the 15th century Portugal established trading posts in west Africa and began selling black slaves, mainly in Iberia and Italy. In the early 16th century, Italy, Portugal, and Spain had cities where black slaves made up 5–10% of

---

[3] Many converted for political reasons, but behind the scenes, they maintained Jewish or Islamic beliefs. These were the crypto-Catholics, and it was important to keep this a secret.

[4] A historian of Catholicism, Professor Agostino Borromeo, of Sapienza University in Rome has estimated that the number killed through the Spanish Inquisition, which excludes unofficial tribunals, was about 12,500. The total number killed, including unofficial tribunals, has been variously estimated to be between 30,000 and 300,000.

[5] It was not really the Roman Catholics versus the Protestants. It was the Roman Catholic Habsburgs, versus anyone supporting the fall of the Habsburgs.

[6] Some International Relations' writers attribute the origin of the nation-state to the Peace of Westphalia (1648), while others vigorously contest this. Generally, it is accepted that the term did originate and develop in Europe. In 19th century Europe, widespread movements emerged to create independent sovereign nation-states. People were tired of being trampled on by the latest conquerors. Nation-states were viewed as having homogenous populations, and it was accepted that homogeneity had to be developed. Once independent, institutions were built, like schools where language and history could be taught to support a common national identity. A primary motive for developing homogenous populations was to have united populations that could and would defend against foreign conquest.

the populations.[lxxii] An emphasis on blood purity brought slave imports into Europe to a virtual end and black populations began decreasing. [lxxiii]

Europe's general aversion to involuntary servitude, did not apply to its colonies. The colonies were supposed to make money for Europe, and this meant supplying them with labor. Beginning in the 17th century, the Atlantic slave trade had major participation (buyers, transporters, and sellers) from European nations building colonial empires. The trade continued into the 19th century, but slaves from this trade affected diversity in Europe only marginally. Racial homogeneity was prized, and slavery was to be part of history – at least in Europe. Religious and ethnic homogeneity was prized too, but continuous wars in Europe and in the neighboring Russian and Ottoman empires had brought in-nation religious and ethnic diversity.

Religious diversity in the form of large Jewish populations was a problem. In the 19th and 20th centuries, the long history of discrimination against the Jews resulted in the Jewish Question. The question was how to manage the negative perceptions of the Jews. After WWI, the answer became giving Jews a homeland in the Middle East. The defeat of the Ottoman Empire in WWI made the Jews original homeland available to the victors. This land became the League of Nation's Mandate for Palestine and it was earmarked for a Jewish homeland. Unfortunately, the homeland didn't appear until 1948.

Reversing diversity became a European theme in the mid-20th century. In and around WWII, Europe underwent multiple genocidal, and ethnic cleansing campaigns. On a mission to create a racially pure Third Reich several populations viewed as sub-human were targeted. This included Jews, ethnic Slavs, Roma (also called Gypsies), and people of color.[47] Hitler assigned death quotas of 50 to 85% to the Slavic Polish, Ukrainian, Czech, and Belarusian populations. For the Slavic Soviets, his plan called for 30 million to die from starvation. He was stopped but not before making serious quota inroads including 2.6 million Soviet POWs dying from hunger, and killing 17% of the Polish population. [lxxiv]

For Jews and Roma, the goal was complete elimination. Before the Nazis surrendered, as many as 70–80% of Europe's Roma were murdered, and an estimated 5–6 million Jews were exterminated, or 2/3rds of Europe's population. Jewish populations in Poland, Latvia, Lithuania, Hungary, Germany, Austria, Slovakia, Greece, the Netherlands, and Yugoslavia were reduced by 70–90%. Researchers at the Holocaust Memorial Museum in Washington, D.C. have estimated that 15–20 million people were exterminated in Nazi concentration camps.[48]

Croatia, then a region of Yugoslavia, was aligned with Nazi Germany and engaged in genocide on a mission to create a homogenous ethnic and religious population. The Croatian Ustaše targeted Roma, Jews, and Serbs. Many Serbian Eastern Orthodox had the option of converting to Roman Catholicism, the religion of most Croats, or transport to a concentration camp. The number of Serbians murdered has been estimated at between 300,000 and 500,000, or about ten times the number of Jews or Roma, which had much smaller populations.[lxxv] The brutality of the

---

[47] People of color were black and most immigrated from Germany's colony in today's Namibia. The number killed is unknown but estimated to be in the low thousands.

[48] The term Holocaust is generally only used to describe the genocide of 5–6 million Jews.

Ustaše, such as displaying the body parts of victims in storefront windows, has been compared to the savagery of the Nazis.

Diversity was also diminished in and around WWII by voluntary emigration, evacuations, people taking flight, and expulsions. People that couldn't find safety and security in Old World Europe were again coming to the New World. Old World Europe's preference for racial, ethnic and religious homogeneity, insufficient economic opportunities, incessant wars driven by imperial ambitions, drives for colonial wealth, and desires to eliminate troublesome populations generated diversity in the New World from the beginning to the end of the Era of Empire.

In the 18th century, one-third of Portugal's population immigrated to Brazil. Half the population of Ireland immigrated to the United States in the 19th century. In 1945 the United States had more than 50% of the global Jewish population. Most came from Europe.[49] At the end of WWII people of European blood were a majority in almost all forty-nine New World nations.

## Racism and anti-Racism in Europe after 1945
### (See Appendix for list of countries in Western Europe)

After WWII Europe had nearly restored homogeneity. Even after the genocidal deviance of the Croatian Ustaše, Yugoslavia remained a white ethnically diverse country. The Soviet Union, with its 15 republics in Europe and Asia also had a white ethnolinguistically diverse population. That was it for diversely populated countries in Europe. "Thanks to war, occupations, boundary adjustments, expulsions and genocides"[lxxvi] different European countries had erased most diversity in the first half of the 20th century. But they couldn't erase it all and discrimination persisted. Quite astonishingly, Europe couldn't even dispense with discrimination against the Jews. After WWII, Jews faced holocaust deniers, verbal assaults, and vandalism on their houses of worship. European Jews are accused of being Nazis; a reference to their occupation of lands allocated for a Palestinian state.[lxxvii] British historian Tony Judt attributes this ongoing persecution of Jews to a collective amnesia of the Holocaust. People wanted to forget they had participated, supported, or condoned the genocide. But Europeans did not forget the lead perpetrator of WWI or WWII. Germans have faced widespread discrimination across the continent for decades, but cross discrimination among Europe's ethnicities (ethnicism) is quite normal and the origins commonly tie to one or more different wars from the many that plagued the continent for centuries.

It seemed like a *non sequitur* when western European nations began importing diverse populations to facilitate rebuilding a region razed by war. But they did. For some nations, doing this helped lessen the guilt from the genocides of WWII and the histories of conquering and subjugating colonial populations. Britain, France, Holland, and Portugal recruited labor from their present and former colonies in Africa and Asia. Germany and Austria had no colonies after WWII. They recruited

---

[49] Many Jewish immigrants were from the Russian Empire but within present-day Poland.

Muslim guest workers from nearby Turkey. Europe's white, Christian populations were now being mixed with multi-colored African, Asian, Muslim, Hindu, and Buddhist populations. This new receptivity to diverse populations was by no means a complete break with the past. Europeans didn't necessarily see new populations as altering homogeneity because many countries implemented multicultural policies that separated like immigrants and guest workers from nationals.[50] In addition to this, *jus sanguinis*-based citizenship laws in most nations limited possibilities to become citizens.

Some of the greatest diversity was introduced into the homelands of empires, and in particular the two with the largest empires: France and the United Kingdom. The United Kingdom was overwhelmingly Christian and white. It allowed colonials or former colonials in any of the fifty-four British Commonwealth nations to become British citizens. This brought people from all over the world with the greatest numbers coming from Bangladesh, India, Pakistan, Ghana, Kenya, Nigeria, Caribbean nations, and Hong Kong. The United Kingdom was becoming diverse racially and religiously. Increasing discrimination became a cause for concern. Beginning in 1962 multiple new immigration policies curtailed immigration from Commonwealth countries.

France had been reluctant to disband its empire after WWII. To prevent this, they did an end run around the UN Charter and incorporated many of its colonies, most of which were in Africa into the French Union (1946-1958). Citizens of the French Union could and did move to France. Until this time, France was quite homogenous from the perspectives of being white and Christian. The immigrant population doubled in twenty years and most came from Africa. Many were Muslim and they faced an added challenge trying to merge into French society. In 1905 the French passed a law that completely separated church and state. It was motivated by a desire to eliminate the church interfering in state again. Among other things, the law forbids the display of conspicuous religious symbols for any religion. This includes head scarves or veils in public places and private schools. French law also forbids discrimination for any reason,[51] but discrimination laws deal with overt discrimination, not unconscious discrimination. Outside designated places, French Muslims can conspicuously display religious symbols. They do and they report high perceptions of discrimination. Real or not, this suppresses a desire to assimilate. It's a Catch 22 because assimilation can minimize or end discrimination. Most French Muslims instead of integrating have self-imposed multiculturalism and it has not had good outcomes. Most of France's 8.8% Muslim population live in common communities and in poverty.[lxxviii]

Added diversity across Europe was accompanied by increasing discrimination. Many European nations can and did adjust policies to limit immigrants but there was the challenge of what to do with millions of segregated guest workers that never returned to the motherland, and other segregated non-European populations. Voluntary or involuntary multicultural/segregated practices perpetuate differences

---

[50] The rationale for keeping guest workers separate was that they were temporary workers and this allowed them to preserve their cultures. The rationale for keeping immigrants separate was to honor their cultures in contrast to assimilation policies, like those used in the United States.

[51] The secularity law is not discriminatory; it applies to people of all faiths. The law was unsuccessfully challenged in French courts and the European Court for Human Rights.

that strengthen ethnic and religious stereotypes that drive discrimination. In a region with a long and sordid history of religious, ethnic, and racial discrimination, multiculturalism seemed like an ill-conceived practice, and it was. This was particularly so because into the 21st century, many European nations didn't have anti-discriminatory laws beyond those for gender.

Although many European nations were early signatories to the UN Charter and committed to fundamental freedoms for all, it would take until 1991, the dissolution of the Soviet Union, for all to become signatories. But what did this do? It should be clear that anti-discrimination commitments to the UN Charter that were not followed by national laws and enforcement were virtually useless. In Europe, these laws did materialize but they could be slow in coming. In 2000 the European Union issued a directive to compel all member states to pass and enforce anti-discrimination laws that inter alia covered race, religion, age, and national origin.[52] Some have still not complied. For example, Germany did in 2006, but Spain in 2020 had not.

**Rising Muslims populations and neo-fascism.** In the 1980s large unassimilated non-European-ethnic populations were instigating the rise of far-right political parties.[53] Jorg Haider became a rising star in Austrian politics on a platform that was pro-Austrian and anti-immigrant. It was dubbed Austro-fascism. Since WWII, western European governments had endeavored to stop the rise of fascism like neo-Nazism, and this development was disturbing. It was also in the 1980s that far-right neo-fascist Jean-Marie Le Pen, a French polarizing convicted racist politician, gained widespread recognition. His platform had aspects of being anti-Muslim,[54] anti-Semitic, and anti-Roma.

Fascist parties for the most part, remained on the fringes until the 21st century when hundreds of thousands of Muslim refugees began arriving in Europe (the 2015 European migrant crisis) and there were rising incidents of Islamic terrorism. National leaders, first among them German Chancellor Merkel, that welcomed the refugees found some Germans gravitating toward fascist political parties. Multiculturalism had been the policy for Germany's guest worker program. Predictably, it led to discrimination and discontent with minorities in Germany. Now Germany was working quickly to integrate new refugees with language studies and skills training that could lead to employment. Some championed the success of Germany's integration program, but having a job and speaking German as a second language did not provide the identity of a fellow German national, and it didn't stop the rise of anti-immigration parties. The Alternative for Germany, a party that is anti-Islamic, anti-immigration, and has shown indicators of anti-Semitism, became the largest opposition party in the legislature. Sweden, a prized destination for Muslim refugees, also saw the rapid rise of an anti-immigration political party, which became the third largest party in the legislature. A region with long histories of Christian and Muslim conflict, Jewish hatred, and seeing populations as superior or inferior was witnessing the challenges of ending entrenched discriminatory beliefs.

---

[52] A directive on anti-gender discrimination had been passed in 1976 by a EU predecessor organization.
[53] In the United States the term far right as used today would be right of center in Europe. In Europe, far right is associated with neo-Nazism and fascism. In the US, this is the ultra-right.
[54] Most Muslims in France came from former African colonies, and most are black.

Commenting on problems with Muslim populations assimilating in Europe, Ross Douthat, a columnist for the NY Times noted that "Europe and America are different. America not only has a more inclusive national identity than Europe and a stronger tradition of assimilating diverse groups of immigrants, it has greater protection for religion practice, more practice with religious diversity, and its citizens are more religious than Europeans." [lxxix] Islam is seen as posing a threat to European values, while Americans value religious pluralism.

Anti-immigrant political parties also remained on the fringe in the UK, but this was not evident during the European migrant crisis. In 2017 the UK voted to exit the European Union. A survey conducted by British Social Attitudes found that the primary reason was concern over too many immigrants. [lxxx] The British blamed its immigrant "problem" on the EU's free movement of people. Exiting the EU was seen as a solution. Were EU nationals the anti-immigrant driver? The rise of Islamic terror is considered a significant cause of the UK's rising xenophobia, so is the real or perceived failures of Muslims to assimilate, and the perceived threat Islam poses to British values. [lxxxi] The UK's Muslim population had doubled in the past decade to 4.4%, but very few were EU nationals. [lxxxii]

Some Muslims have supported Islamic terrorism in Europe. In part, Muslims rationalized the actions because they supported the aim of terrorizing infidels viewed as marginalizing them. [lxxxiii] Violent retribution for real or perceived discrimination might make some Muslims feel better, but it is completely ineffective at lessening discrimination. To the contrary, it has been proven to increase it. [lxxxiv] This would be particularly strong in Europe, where nations are founded on rule of law. Since 2015 there have been more than ten mass terrorism incidents targeting white European Christians. This has strengthened the stereotype of Muslims as dangerous religious zealots that are hell bent on destroying the Christian way of life. Islamophobia has been fueled and refueled. Even without terrorism, solving real or perceived discrimination against Muslims is a tall order in the region once called Christendom. Christian values are seen as quite different from Muslim values, for example religiosity v secularity, and the faiths share a long history of conflicts that included enslavement, subordination, ethnic cleansing, massacres, confiscation of assets, and land annexations. Without integration, discrimination against Muslims may be as hard to end as discrimination against Christians is in MENA. Maybe not. Nations in MENA do not encourage the integration of non-Muslims, but European governments do. There have been varying degrees of success. Laws can curtail overt discrimination, but they are pretty useless when it comes to unconscious biases. Mutual animosities that drive unconscious biases have been built up over centuries and they are not going to disappear because governments pass laws.

In a survey on perceptions of discrimination in Britain, Muslims that are Bengalis and Pakistanis, were found to perceive the highest levels of discrimination. These are dark-skinned populations but so are blacks and Indians, and perceptions for these two groups were much lower. It's entirely reasonable in Islamophobic Christendom that perceptions of discrimination are higher for Muslims than non-Muslims and that biases are mutual. [lxxxv]

France has Europe's largest black population and its largest Muslim population. [55] (The two populations overlap.) If having the largest populations of blacks and

Muslims conjures up an image of racial tolerance, France also comes out on top for hiring discrimination against non-white minorities. Sweden placed second of nine countries evaluated. Researchers were surprised that five out of seven European nations scored worse than the United States,[56] and one scored the same. It had been assumed that any nation with a history of in-country slavery would score as more discriminatory against blacks. Also surprising, the study found no statistical difference in discrimination against non-white minority populations.[lxxxvi]

**The Atlantic slave trade.** About 1/3rd of British blacks (about 600,000) are Afro-Caribbean and descendants of slaves from the Atlantic trade. French blacks are predominantly descended from former French colonies in Africa. The relatively minor presence of descendants from the Atlantic trade in Europe can conceal the dominant role of European parties in the trade. In descending order of the number of slaves transported they include Portugal, Britain, Spain, France, the Netherlands and Denmark.[57] It can also conceal that for most or all of the period when slavery was legal in Europe's colonies, most slaves and slaveholders from the Atlantic trade were "subjects" of European empires. Unlike the United States, there has been relatively little discourse in Europe about its roles in the trade. Portugal has been contemplating a monument to the 5.8 million slaves it ferried to the New World Americas, but there is plenty of resistance. Portugal relishes its colonial history. It was a time when it shared the global stage with much larger European nations. It also sees itself as less racist, even though it transported more slaves and held its colonies longer than any other European nation.[lxxxvii]

Britain transported 3.1 million African slaves, and most went to its colonies in the Caribbean. They also supplied most of the slaves that went to the Thirteen Colonies. In 1835, 46 thousand slave owners were British. Most rented their slaves and never lived in the colonies. Still, you don't hear much about Britain's role in the slave trade. "Few acts of collective forgetting have been as thorough and as successful as the erasing of slavery from Britain's island story."[lxxxviii] What instead is remembered is Britain's role in successfully patrolling the seas from 1807-1867 [58] to intercept slave ships on a mission to end the trade. France, which carried about 1.3 million slaves and mostly to its colonies in the Caribbean, is also accused of collective amnesia on its role in the slave trade. The same can be said of Spain.

In the 21st century some have unsuccessfully tried to raise the profile of Europe's role in slavery. The challenge may be that slavery is one issue among many others that viewed with a modern lens are troubling, like hundreds of years of wars of conquest, reverse hierarchies, massacres, genocides, some heinous religious discrimination, and mercantilism. These actions affected blacks, whites, Asians and indigenous populations all over the world during Europe's five centuries competing for global supremacy. If Europeans were to turn the history clock back a couple

---

[55] France does not collect statistics on race or ethnicity. France is believed to numerically have the largest black populations in Europe (7%). The UK is second with 3.5%. France's Muslim population is about 8.5%. Germany and the UK are second. About 6% of their populations are Muslim.

[56] Only Germany had a lower rating than the US.

[57] About 1% of slaves from the Atlantic slave trade were brought to the Americas by US enterprises. A portion of these slaves were sold in the United States.

[58] In 1808 when the US outlawed banned the trade, they joined Britain to help end the slave trade. Their role was substantive, but with a much smaller Navy its role was minor.

centuries further, there would be the uncomfortable truth that 3/4ths of the population were serfs. Serfdom replaced slavery in the 12th and 13th centuries and persisted into the 16th century in Western Europe, and the 19th century in Central Europe.[lxxxix] History without the context of the time period has so many chapters that shock today's conscience. Evaluating history without context would doom every nation in the world to living with perpetual guilt for the actions of ancestors behaving consistent with the time.

**Challenges managing diversity and discrimination.** The growth in fascist political parties led Chancellor Merkel to pronounce multiculturalism a failure.[xc] What though was the solution? Not all European countries practice multiculturalism. The UK, France, and Denmark, for example, have encouraged integration but not all diverse people want to integrate. It's very common for black and brown people and Muslims of any color to prefer to live in ethnic communities, self-implement multiculturalism, and reject values and even languages of the host country or adopted homeland. This inadvertently cross-perpetuates discrimination between the majority and minorities. The majority want minorities to integrate, and minorities can resent and even reject this. Minorities can further resent relatively poorer living conditions. This the majority resents because: they see the refusal of minorities to integrate as a big reason they have lower paying jobs; they see minorities ungratefully benefitting from rich social welfare programs that often elevate their lifestyles; and they take umbrage at immigrants using newfound protected freedoms, like freedom of speech to disparage them as racists and infidels, and even organize acts of terror.

Diversity in Europe began increasing after WWII. Once white and Christian, it now has more diversity, although it does remain overwhelmingly white and Christian. Many people that are not white or Christian face real or perceived discrimination. Between overt and covert discrimination, the former is easier to address. The EU and most European nations have laws to punish forms of racism and xenophobia in the workplace, education, healthcare, social security, and when accessing goods and services. Anti-discrimination laws are, however, generally incapable of addressing unconscious biases, or faulty perceptions. [59] Laws cannot regulate what people think, and in democracies much of what people say is protected by free speech.

The challenges the EU's anti-discrimination policies face are complicated again for two reasons. While Europe is reasonably racially and religiously homogenous; it is incredibly diverse ethnically. The EU is not the United States of Europe. Beginning in 1993 European nations joined forces in the European Union (EU). A group of twenty-seven nations, just as many cultures and nearly as many languages have merged. A principal motivation was to increase the economic output of the bloc to better compete with large economies like the United States and China. This merger is not and never will be a cultural merger, and it cannot conceal long seated historical animosities, and the conflict between the richer ethnicities in the north and

---

[59] The 2000 EU anti-discrimination directive includes protection for indirect discrimination. This covers disparate impact. These are practices that have a greater effect on a group of individuals without overtly targeting them. It has been seen as having connections to unconscious discrimination. In the US, practices that have a disparate discriminatory impact are also illegal.

the poorer ethnicities in the south and east. One stated reason for the UK to undergo the painful process of EU extraction is they wanted to put an end to the free movement of people from EU member states, particularly from the east. Ethnically diverse white Christians discriminating against white Christians has been a long-standing European tradition; the EU won't change that anytime soon.

The second complication is that Europe is reasonably new to having diverse racial and religious populations and anti-discrimination laws. After WWII, Europe was racially and religiously homogenous, and this was not an accident. The year 1945 was a tipping point. But it takes time, and history shows that it takes a lot of time, for people to adjust to new populations. Different values, different appearances, and different behaviors send up caution flags. National policies that welcome immigrants, and laws that prohibit discrimination are not magic fairy dust that make new fears and entrenched biases passed down for many generations disappear.

Europe's anti-discrimination commitment is strong. It's long historical preference for national populations that are homogenous racially, ethnically, and religiously adds extra challenges that will slowly be lessened over time.

## European Overseas Empires – Old World (pre-1945)

The creation of overseas colonial empires was uniquely European. So was the creation of empires that spanned the Old and New Worlds. The Chinese, Islamic, and Russians built their empires by conquering contiguous land polities in the Old World.[1] Only the Europeans built far-flung empires that involved conquests and colonization on all six inhabitable continents: Old-World Africa, Asia, and Europe; and New-World Oceania, North America, and South America.

When it came to diversity, Europeans prized homogeneity at home, but they placed no premium on this in their New or Old-World colonies. Colonies existed to deliver economic benefits for the motherlands of empires. When unskilled labor was needed, it was generally secured from cost-effective sources wherever. This added diversity. Following right behind was discrimination.

Most of Europe's Old-World colonies came into being in the 19th century, and most had adequate indigenous unskilled labor. Because slavery was in the process of being abolished in Europe's empires, any needs for additional labor were mostly fulfilled by free labor and indentured servants from China and India. Chinese free laborers gained a reputation in Southeast Asia for being industrious, inexpensive workers. This made them popular with profit-minded colonial administrators, but less popular with indigenous populations that preferred homogeneity and a captive audience for their services. Whether they were industrious or average workers, the Chinese and Indians faced discrimination everywhere they worked outside their homelands. Discrimination could be racial/ethnic, racial and religious, or just because they were foreign.

There wasn't a need for unskilled labor in the Middle East, but the Arab slave trade continued delivering slaves here until 1962. It was embarrassing to the British that protectorates and mandates in MENA were still using slave labor even after WWII ended.[li, xci]After all, one of the primary responsibilities of mandate oversight was to guarantee the rights of racial minorities. How though were British overseers going to give rights to slaves? Elevating black slaves to equality with light-skinned Arabs would have shown an intolerable level of cultural and historical ignorance.

When defining borders, European empires created diverse states that often promoted discrimination. Borders in sub-Saharan colonies commonly encircled very diverse populations. Too often this included tribes with long histories of enslaving nearby tribes. Nigeria's borders enclosed more than 240 distinct ethnic groups. Borders for several sub-Saharan nations, including Nigeria, had a Muslim-majority population in the north and mostly Christian and indigenous religious populations in the south. For more than a thousand years Muslims had been enslaving non-Muslims in this region and now they lived as co-colonials.

The borders Britain oversaw for Iraq merged three populations that lived peacefully in geographically separate administrative divisions in the Ottoman Empire. They were separated for a reason. In Iraq, the populations remained segregated, but the minority Arabic-speaking, historically superior Sunnis became the rulers. Like many diverse nations in Africa, Iraq was built on a diverse and delicate foundation that without fundamental freedoms for all, and the integration of diverse populations would descend into discriminatory chaos. It turns out multiple times.

Most skilled and government administrative jobs in Europe's colonies in Africa and Asia were carried out by white Europeans and this left a bad taste. It may not have been that white administrators were worse than locals. Indeed, local rulers that followed often proved they were not. But they were a minority white population subjugating the majority. Even if the Europeans brought progress, subordination to whites was always resented and their actions were seen as racist. Minimally they were benevolently racist.

## Racism and anti-Racism after 1945
(See Appendix for lists of countries in each Old-World Region)

European colonies were present in every Old-World region. In this section there are breakouts for Central Europe, Southeast Asia, sub-Saharan Africa, and South Asia.

**Sub-Saharan Africa**. Everyone that faces discrimination hates it. But when the tables are turned, turnabout can be seen as fair play. This has been a common story in sub-Saharan Africa. In 1821, the nation of Liberia was created by an organization in the United States as a home where free blacks could live absent discrimination and turn the chapter on slavery. About 12,000 free American blacks migrated to Liberia. An American black declared independence in 1847. He made sure racism would not be a problem, at least not for blacks; only blacks are permitted to be citizens.[xcii] Provisions were also made to make sure slavery would not be a problem. In their constitution, slavery is forbidden. Every Liberian was black, free, and presumably equal. Maybe not. Former US slaves became a political elite class ruling a nation that enslaved indigenous people. According to an investigation and report by the League of Nations in 1930 [xciii] it was not classic slavery with slave markets and dealers, because the Liberian constitution prohibited this. And it was not "classic" from a view of slavery as whites buying and selling blacks, or Muslims buying and selling non-Muslims. This was black on black slavery and the methods that were used were common to regions of Africa, for example, pawning.

> "Pawning was a native West-African custom whereby a person, usually a child relative, was given to a third party in servitude for an indefinite period…This system was being abused in order to circumvent the constitutional prohibition against slavery…the only distinction between the two was the passing of a token -a leopards tooth for a free-born and a piece of metal or mat for a born slave… One headman pawned two sons in order to pay a fine for "road delinquencies"…Another pawned his wife and child to pay a fine." [xciv]

There were "oppressive conditions analogous to slavery, forced labor for public purpose, [and] forced labor for private enterprise." In some cases, the government supplied forced labor to work on plantations in other African nations. In 1953 Liberia agreed to abolish slavery but it was still fiddling with nomenclature. In 1962 it strengthened laws to put an end to the existing practice of the government supplying forced labor.

Americo-Liberians ruled until 1980. The failure of Americo-Liberians to extend "liberty and equality to the indigenous populations"[xcv] was the real trigger behind two civil wars that engulfed Liberia between 1989 and 2005. The wars pitted members of different tribes that were anxious to enjoy the privileges of a "ruling class," like the Americo-Liberians.

Some African tribes/ethnic groups have experienced heinous and covert discrimination that has persisted into the 21st century. The Aro Confederacy (1690-1902) predominantly located in southern Nigeria fueled its economy with the delivery of about 3.5 million slaves to buyers in the Atlantic slave trade.[xcvi] The largest group of the enslaved were people born as slaves from the Igbo tribe. Some enslavers were "freeborn" Igbo,[60] but there were Africans from many different tribes involved in "the business" of supplying slaves. As one woman described it, it took courage to capture slaves.

> "Our people traded extensively in slaves. It was a dangerous trade, but very profitable. It was dangerous, because you must be strong enough to overpower your victim. Secondly, you must be prepared to risk your life, wresting children from their parents, and so on. In fact, slaves were obtained in various ways - by kidnapping, through wars, through punishment for crimes and breach of taboos, for failure to pay debts.[61] Parents even sold their children, for want of food." One "man had to sell two of his children in exchange for the Ozo title… another man had so many children, and he had to ask them to buy one of his

---

[60] The Igbo had a caste system. There were free people, captives or debt slaves (ohu) , domestic slaves (osu), and slaves sacrificed to vicious deities (ume).

[61] According to Koelle's informants 40% of slaves were kidnapped or seized, 24% war captives, 19% tricked by a friend or relative, and 19% by judicial sentences.

children in exchange for one cow... The slave dealers, mostly Aro
people [an Igbo subgroup]" would exchange European goods for the
children. Nkwonto Nwuduaku in Urunnebo, October 16, 1974[xcvii]

Another added: "The successful sale of adults was considered an
exploit for which a man was hailed by praise singers, akin to exploits
in wrestling, war, or in hunting animals like the lion." [xcviii]

The end of the Atlantic slave trade in the 19th century led to a glut of Igbo slaves.
"Those [African] families which were really rich competed with one another in the
number of slaves each killed for its dead or used to placate the gods." [xcix]

When the British colonized Nigeria in 1901, they were determined to end slavery,
particularly among the Igbo. For the British to end slavery, they had to successfully
wage war with the Aro Confederacy, which they did. But this was abolition by
British fiat, and it was ignored by many. There were long-standing traditions where
some people were born slaves. Legal slavery persisted in parts of Nigeria until an
agreement to abolish it in 1961. But laws, that conflict with traditions always
experience difficulties with enforcement.

In the Nigerian Civil (Biafran) War (1967–1970), an estimated one to three
million Igbo died, most from the government's use of a humanmade famine that
today is considered genocide. [ix] Eight to thirty thousand Igbo were massacred in anti-
Igbo pogroms in 1966. Discrimination against the Igbo persisted. In the 1990s
Nigerian Chief Alex Akinyele said: "There are so many marginalized groups in
Nigeria, but the case of the Ndigbo [Igbo] is too obvious. They are more
marginalized than the others." [x, 62] Three out of four Igbo castes are for slaves, and
many Nigerians still see them and treat them as slaves. They are called osu (or ohu),
which means slave. [c] In 2018 the Igbo caste system was being abolished by
agreement one village at a time.

The last nations in the world to officially abolish slavery were in North Africa
and sub-Saharan Africa. In 1973 Mali became the last sub-Saharan nation to agree to
abolish slavery, but slavery continued to be practiced with impunity, and not just in
Mali. Fourteen nations in this region have tribes/ethnic groups that still hierarchically
order people using caste systems where people inherit their status and often their
professions. People are born, recognized by self and others, and die as inferior or
superior. In some, the lowest caste is a slave caste.[ci] Where slavery has been
abolished, descendants of slaves can face discrimination. They can be prevented
from merging and marrying "freeborn" people. [cii]

In some nations slavery that is compliant with Islamic religious law (sharia)
continues, and there are still instances of enslaving people captured in conflict.
Slavery in Africa is often portrayed as a gentler kinder form than existed in the New
World. In the 21st century being born inferior and shunned by others because they
fear a polluting influence doesn't sound gentle or kind. Slavery legally existed in
many parts of Africa for more than a millennia before the Atlantic slave trade began,

---

[62] It is estimated that British slave ships transported about 60,000 Igbo slaves to Maryland and Virginia.
Igbos represent about 15% of the total slaves sold in the US. During the Biafran War, an undefined
number of Igbos migrated to the United States.

and for 150 years after European empires began abolishing the trade. Today it persists and continues to be condoned in some areas. It's probably apparent that views toward slavery differ in some parts of the world.

Most nations in sub-Saharan Africa became independent in the 1960s. As a general rule, once they became sovereign nations, they strongly encouraged non-black populations to leave. This included Europeans, South Asians, and Arabs. This occurred even though many managed important political and economic roles for which there were no local replacements. Biracial populations were permitted to stay but subjugated to black populations. Previously, blacks were subjugated to mulattoes. [63]

Sub-Saharan Africa was again Black Africa, a region of indigenous populations. The borders for sub-Saharan African nations were a construct of European empires creating colonial boundaries at the tail end of the 19th century during the African carve up.[64] At independence, African leaders agreed to keep the borders intact to reduce the possibility of endless wars. But there have been endless wars. Most, however, are not inter-nation.

Being white in Europe is not a homogenous marker, neither is being black in Africa. Like Europe, borders in Africa amalgamated diverse tribal/ethnic groups. But while European states created homogeneity from diversity through the development of nationalities, the same is generally not true in sub-Saharan nations. Ethnically diverse, lacking an integrated nationality, and absent anti-discrimination laws or other commitments is a perfect storm for unchecked discrimination.

Almost all discrimination in sub-Saharan Africa is black on black; it is inter- and intra-tribal and -ethnic. Racism in Africa is most commonly ethnicism. Initially many new national leaders appealed to their diverse populations with messages of unity, but not for long. It became evident that the key to holding power (and wealth) was to divide and rule or said another way to discriminate and rule. National leaders surrounded themselves with people from their tribe or ethnic group. These became the people of privilege. Endemic corruption ensured their loyalty. For everyone else there was discrimination, and this could take lethal forms. When a new leader arrived in office from a different tribe or ethnic group the preferred and discriminated populations changed. Some unpreferred populations were made stateless.

Competition for national office, and the spoils it offered was intense among tribal/ethnic groups. Coups and civil wars became common. In the 1980s the chance of a successful coup d'état in Africa was 60%.[ciii] During the Cold War (1945-1991) there were about two hundred successful and attempted coups.[civ] Between 1970 and 2005 there were more than forty civil wars. The outcomes of successful coups or

---

[63] Today, white minorities are less than 0.5% in 75% of African nations. The largest white populations are in southern Africa, where whites continued ruling in South Africa and Zimbabwe until 1991 and 1978 respectively. White populations in South Africa are 8.9% (down from 21%), Namibia with 6% (down from 14%) and Botswana and Eswatini with 3%. Zimbabwe's white population is 0.2% (down from 7%).

[64] The Berlin Conference (1884–1885) was a meeting of European powers and the Russian Empire to carve-up the African continent into colonies. Rationales for doing this included ending slavery, halting the spread of Islam, and a civilization mission.

civil wars were superior and victorious populations, and inferior and defeated populations.

Ethnic rivals for national power could engage in ethnic cleansing and genocide. Idi Amin arrived in Uganda via a coup in 1971. Amin's government was filled with members of his Kakwa ethnic group and neighboring ethnicities. To prevent a resurgence of his predecessor, Amin ordered mass killings of his predecessor's tribe. In Rwanda and Burundi competition for power between Hutus and Tutsis resulted in multiple genocides. In 1972 Tutsis in Burundi targeted the elimination of Hutus. In 1994 Rwandan Hutus targeted the elimination of Tutsis. To minimize any further horrifying outcomes, Rwanda's Hutus and Tutsis are being forcibly assimilated. [cv] Will it work?

Nations in this region still uproot semi-nomadic indigenous populations to make way for endeavors to support national economies. The Samburu and Maasai of Kenya and Tanzania have been forcibly displaced to make way for tourism. [cvi] The pygmies count among the oldest inhabitants of sub-Saharan Africa. They have faced forced evictions without compensation, and more recently ethnic cleansing and cannibalism.[cvii, cviii] Between 1997 and 2005 the Bushman of southern Africa, one of the oldest living people in the world were forcibly uprooted.[cix] Nomadic lifestyles for some indigenous populations have left them stateless. Like indigenous populations in many parts of the world there is a lack of fundamental freedoms like protection from exploitation and arbitrary actions of the state.

Almost all nations in sub-Saharan Africa were colonized by the Europeans following the Berlin Conference (1884-1885). One exception was South Africa. It was colonized by the Dutch in 1652. It later became a British colony (1806-1961). South Africa was an original signatory of the UN Charter, committed to equal freedoms for all.[65] Contrary to this commitment, in 1948 the ruling white minority cemented a lock on power and prosperity with an apartheid policy (racial segregation). Millions of blacks were uprooted from their homes and transported to black-only "nations," millions were imprisoned, and blacks were disenfranchised. [cx] Apartheid ended in 1991. The new President, Nelson Mandela, was committed to building a rainbow nation where all were treated equally. His successors, not as much.

South Africa has a legal anti-discrimination commitment to all people, but there are plenty of ways to conceal racist policies and practices. For example, the government is more likely to investigate and punish whites that engage in racist communications than blacks. A 2017 study on media and government responses to incidents of racist communications found the government "aggravating the situation by cracking down on white nobodies while allowing black somebodies to go scot-free."[cxi] Currently South Africa is considering an amendment to its constitution to expropriate large plots of farmland without compensation. Like America's Black Codes, the amendment is colorblind, but the people affected are white.

Addressing discrimination is not a priority for most nations in this region, and in many cases, it is not recognized as a problem. Pervasiveness notwithstanding. When issues of discrimination are recognized, it is common to point a finger of blame at

---

[65] Liberia was also a founding nation. The only other independent or virtually independent African nations were Libya and Ethiopia, and both were occupied wholly or in part in 1945.

white European slave traders or colonizers. African involvement in the slave trades, like Arab involvement is commonly censored. Inconvenient truths often are. For most African nations colonization lasted 60-70 years, but some forms of discrimination like slavery, tribal hierarchies, and caste systems that pigeonhole people as inferior at birth have been in place for thousands of years. Even today, all are present and accepted in reduced forms. Black on black discrimination seems normal, natural and may be viewed as helpful. If it is seen as problematic, it is not given a lot of time or attention outside coups and civil wars. But these have created new discriminatory problems.

**Central Europe**. Collective amnesia on the Holocaust also infiltrated Central Europe. The Holocaust reduced Central Europe's Jewish population by 82 percent. After 1945, Jews remained unwelcome. In the immediate aftermath, Jews faced pogroms in five Central European nations and 55 years later Jews were 1.5% of their 1939 population. Discrimination remains intense in multiple countries, but it is equally intense for Muslims.[cxii] Muslims have lived in this region since the 15th century. Most are moderate and protected by religious freedom and anti-discrimination laws, but where Muslims are a minority, discrimination is often unpersuaded by illegality.

Central Europe was center stage during the competition for global supremacy. European, Islamic and Russian/Soviet empires ruled all or parts of this region. Diversity was not an outcome of labor needs but lots of empire-directed population transport, encouraged religious conversions, and border changes. Some polities became really diverse.

The borders for Yugoslavia were carved from the Ottoman and Austria-Hungary empires in 1918.[66] The population was not remotely homogenous, but creating a defensible nation required size and many ethnolinguistic groups in this area were small. Yugoslavia's position was not unique. Many European nations seeking size had combined diverse white ethnolinguistic groups. But afterward, they created homogeneity from diversity by building nationalities where people shared the bonds of language, religion, and common values. Integrating populations is never simple. In the case of Yugoslavia, it was really complicated, but it was also never seriously addressed. It stayed a multicultural state. There were large segregated populations of Roman Catholics and Eastern Orthodox that were ethnically Serbian, Croat and Macedonian, in addition to Sunni, Shiite, and Sufi Muslims that were Bosnian and Albanian.

Czechoslovakia merged Czech and Slovak ethnolinguistic groups, in addition to German-speaking Bohemians (called Sudeten Germans). All were white. The groups remained segregated.[67] Instead of creating the elements of a common nationality, it stayed a segregated multicultural state. Less than seventy-five years after independence Czechoslovakia became two nations. Around the same time Yugoslavia imploded into a sea of ethnic and religious conflict that would result in seven nations. During the Yugoslav Wars (1991-2001) non-Croats in Croatia, and non-Serbs in Serbia were targeted for removal. In newly independent Bosnia Herzegovina, Bosnian Serb forces targeted Bosnian Muslims (Bosniaks) and Croats

---

[66] In 1918 the name was the Kingdom of Serbs, Croats and Slovenes.
[67] The Sudeten Germans were expelled after WWII.

for elimination. Labeled the Bosnian genocide, 100,000 Bosnians were killed. Eighty percent were Bosniaks.

All of the successor states of Czechoslovakia and Yugoslavia are members or trying to become members of the European Union. All of their people have fundamental freedoms, and their nations have commitments to anti-discrimination.

**Southeast Asia.** Chinese and Indians filled most additional needs for unskilled labor in Europe's colonies in Southeast Asia. Many of their descendants remained. In Malaysia, the indigenous Muslim-majority Malays have maintained a superior position over the significant non-Muslim Chinese and Indian minority populations. Constitutionally Malays are entitled to favored treatment in many central facets of life, like government services, education, and housing. Not all Muslim Malays feel privileged. As of 1996, Shiite Muslims have been formally considered deviant, and prohibited from proselytizing (trying to convert others to their faith).[cxiii] They have faced regular bouts of persecution. In Muslim-majority Brunei Darussalam (Brunei), Malays are citizens, and most others are not. Most Bruneian-born Chinese, about 15% of the population, are stateless. Oil-rich Brunei has rich social welfare programs, but stateless people receive substandard educations and health care and are forbidden from owning property or businesses. In western parlance both of these nations are racist. but they see it differently. They are reinforcing and preserving the social superiority of Muslim Malays. People that don't like it can leave, and many have.

The Chinese have also faced severe discrimination in Indonesia, Vietnam, Laos, and Cambodia. Beginning in 1975 images of Vietnamese boat people filled the news hours in western nations. Most were ethnic Chinese. Some 450,000 ethnic Chinese were expelled or fled when the Vietnam War ended. In Cambodia, 2-300,000 "wealthy" Chinese were murdered between 1975 and 1979. More recently in Cambodia, discrimination against Chinese stems from the perception or reality of superior-minded Chinese investors and workers, and the fear of Chinese cultural appropriation. It's not a baseless fear. During the Chinese Empire, nations in Southeast Asia had to regularly pay tribute to acknowledge Chinese superiority.

Was it the commercial success of the Chinese, or discrimination that drove legislation in Indonesia (1998) summarized as Chinese cultural genocide? The legislation was recalled, however, prior to this there were multiple violent and deadly discriminatory episodes. Ethnic Chinese continue to face discrimination here and throughout this region. Rising China re-exerting superiority, for example, by encroaching on land and seas in Southeast Asia is not helpful to lessening discrimination.

At independence in 1948 Buddhist-majority Myanmar[68] was on a mission to create a homogenous Burmese nation. An early initiative was the expulsion of Indians, many of which held important positions in the government and the economy during British rule. Next up was creating a common Burmese nationality among Myanmar's diverse ethno-linguistic and religious groups in its Frontier Areas.[69] Everyone was being forced to adopt the Burmese language and culture, including the

---

[68] Burma was renamed Myanmar in 1989.
[69] The Frontier Areas were administered separately under British rule. At independence all areas were ruled by Burma's central government.

Buddhist religion. The grandest resistance came from Christians, Muslims, and Hindus that refused to convert. An estimated 800,000 were incarcerated. Amnesty international said the tactics used in these detention centers resembled those of KGB pre-trial detention camps where "prisoners" were made to stand for hours in windowless rooms smaller than a phone booth. The Rohingyas, a Muslim population in the Frontier Areas, tried to organize for independence. Most had their citizenship revoked in 1982. In 2015, when external militants terrorized government soldiers and policemen on behalf of the Rohingyas, the response from the government was swift and severe. Today most Rohingyas live as refugees in neighboring Bangladesh. At nearly one million, they are the largest stateless population in the world.

Discrimination against minorities in this region is rampant and seen as normal. For many it begins at birth and perseveres until death.[70] It's unlikely to change anytime soon because majorities see discrimination as ensuring their rightful place. Malaysia, Brunei, and Myanmar have legalized discrimination, while others condone it. According to the World Values Survey, nations in this region count among the most intolerant, although not as intolerant as South Asia or MENA.[71]

**South Asia.** South Asia is another region where religionism remains the primary form of racism, and quite a bit of it is legal and state sponsored.

British India was the only Hindu-majority colony colonized by an Islamic empire before colonization by a European empire. Religion was of paramount importance to governing and ordering populations in the Mughal Empire, but not in the 19th century British Empire, at least not from the government's perspective. In British India, Hindus and Muslims were equal. To Muslims, equality with Hindu polytheists, and having national laws prioritized over Islamic religious law was an insult to Islam and a giant social plunge. Some dissatisfied Muslims developed Islamic revival movements and called for jihad by the sword.[72, cxiv] For the Hindu majority, the Muslim rejection of equality heightened tensions that had been brewing from eleven centuries of repeated bouts of sharia-sanctioned persecution and conquest. Riots between Hindus and Muslims became constant. To the British this conflict was irreconcilable and ultimately led to the decision to partition British India into India and Pakistan in 1947. Pakistan was to be a nation for Muslims, and India was to be a nation for all religions, but clearly with a Hindu majority. Both were to be secular.

The partition triggered a spontaneous mass migration. Hindus feared persecution living in a Muslim-ruled country and vice versa. An estimated 14 million cross-migrated, and over a million died. The migration exacerbated tensions between Muslims and Hindus. The conflict partition was meant to resolve had instead made it worse. Now cross-discrimination was inter-nation, and intra- and inter-religious, and this remains today.

Intra-religious and inter-religious discrimination permeated the Bangladesh War for independence (1971). The Punjabi-speaking Muslims of West Pakistan instigated

---

[70] Singapore is an exception. They have been endeavoring to deliver equal freedoms to all. Like others in this region, they have an ethnic Chinese, Malay, Indian population mix, but with a Chinese majority.
[71] Tolerance or intolerance in sub-Saharan Africa is unknown because survey participation has been minor and inconclusive.
[72] Jihad, which literally means struggling can pertain to internal, external, and personal struggles. Jihad by the sword means a struggle carried out with weapons.

the war by discriminating against Pakistan's majority Bengali-speaking Muslims of East Pakistan. During the war the West Pakistani military targeted Bengali intelligentsia and Bengali men, and singled out Hindus. Many consider these actions genocide and gendercide (of men).[cxv, cxvi] Hindu homes were marked with yellow H's so the army would know they were special targets.[cxvii,cxviii] It has been estimated that out of 10 million refugees in this war, 8 million were Hindus from East Pakistan. Even after independence, Hindus residing in newly named Bangladesh experienced severe discrimination. In 1947 Hindus were about 31% of the population. In 1971 they were 20% and 8% in 2011.

Hindus have also faced severe discrimination in Buddhist-majority Bhutan. In 1990 most of the Hindus, about 16% of the population, lost their citizenship.[73] Some were expulsed while others stayed in Bhutan stateless. Some had their property destroyed and were victims of torture. These actions were supported by the King of Bhutan who said, "Bhutan cannot afford the luxury of such diversity which may impede the growth of social harmony and unity among its people." [cxix]

Most Hindus in Buddhist-majority Sri Lanka were similarly forced into statelessness at independence in 1948. The response from the Hindu Tamils led to twenty-six years of civil war. During this time about one million Tamils permanently vacated the island nation. Many were repatriated to India. Today, Hindu Tamils that continued living in Sri Lanka are citizens and the nation has been progressing its laws to deliver equal fundamental freedoms to Buddhists, Christians, Hindus and Muslims. However, twenty-six recent years of war makes it non-trivial to expunge conscious and unconscious discrimination. Three deadly terror attacks perpetrated by local Muslim groups in 2019, have complicated further the process of addressing discrimination in any form against Muslims. For the Tamils, things are actually worse in India. India generally welcomes persecuted Hindus, but Sri Lankan Tamils are an exception. They have faced discrimination that was accentuated in 2019 when they were excluded from a new law that permits a path to citizenship for legal non-Muslim refugees.

Hindus that remained in Pakistan after partition have met with discrimination and outright hatred. Some hatred is taught. Public school textbooks until 2011 encouraged hatred against non-Muslims. Most children that attend school, attend religious educational schools and they are taught that polytheism, a belief of Hinduism, is an unforgivable sin. At independence Hindus made up 15-20% of Pakistan's population. In 2015 it was 1%. One percent that were denied food and daily essentials during the Covid-19 pandemic.[cxx]

Pakistan's founder Muhammad Ali Jinnah made it clear that Hindus, Christians, and Muslims were all Pakistani and would enjoy equal rights.[cxxi] But, Jinnah was long gone. Pakistan had become a nation where anyone non-Muslim, and some Muslims faced discrimination. After 1979, Muslims that didn't follow the Sunni Deobandi movement [74] could face discrimination, and this could take deadly forms. In 2012, according to Human Rights Watch, attacks against Christians and Hindus

---

[73] In the early 20th century in neighboring Hindu-majority Nepal, Buddhist monks were twice deported *en masse*.
[74] The Taliban in Afghanistan follow the Deobandi movement.

reached an unprecedented level. These attacks though were fewer than those against non-Deobandi Muslims of which Shias figured prominently.

Slavery in Pakistan was only legally abolished in 1992, but it persists from one generation to the next. Most are Hindu Dalits. These Dalits have not only inherited their lowly status at birth but also the debts of their parents. (The Dalits are covered below.) An estimated 3 million children and adults are bonded laborers caught in an escapable cycle of working for all controlling landlords.

Hindus and Shias also face severe discrimination in Afghanistan. In the 1970s Hindus were estimated to number 700,000. Now they are about 7,000. An exodus began following the Soviet-Afghan war (1979-1989). Land confiscations by the Muslim mujahedeen made it clear to Hindus that they were not wanted.[cxxii] Shiite Muslims, about 20% of the population, also found a new discriminatory reality. Outside a genocide in 1900, they faced discrimination but lived in "relative" peace prior to Taliban rule in 1996. This is no longer true. Shias face blatant discrimination, including many incidents of mass casualties. In 2015 Afghan Shias represented the bulk of Europe's 175,000 Afghan refugees, but there are millions that continue to live without peace in Afghanistan, or as refugees in different nations.[cxxiii,cxxiv,cxxv]

In the Maldives discrimination has been institutionalized against anyone not Sunni Muslim. Only Muslims can be citizens and freely practice religion. Only Sunnis can run for office. Guest workers in the Maldives are about half the working population. Most are Sunnis from Bangladesh. Their diminished status is obvious. Guest worker is a euphemism for forced labor. Deplorable working conditions are a problem. [cxxvi]

Hindus generally discriminate against Hindus because all are stratified in a five-level hereditary caste. This includes four castes that represent people of different professions, in addition to the Dalit or untouchables. Located below the strata of caste, the Dalit face extraordinary levels of discrimination.

India abolished untouchability at independence (1947), but the Dalit have been an integral part of India's culture for thousands of years. It wasn't disappearing because politicians abolished it.[75,76] In 1955, India tried to strengthen the laws. It became illegal to restrict access to anyone in public places, or to deny anyone drinking water. Quotas were also established to force proportionate representation in *public* employment and universities.

Discrimination against the Dalit continued to be a major problem. In 1989, parliament passed the Prevention of Atrocities Act to strengthen protections for the Dalit and other discriminated classes of people. The government later conceded that the act was a failure. They found that the police and the judiciary did not enforce the act; conviction rates were about 2-3%. The law was strengthened in 2015, but it too had little impact. The law was not even being applied to enslaved Dalit. In 2016 the Global Slavery Index estimated that tens of millions in this region were enslaved as forced commercial sex workers, child laborers, armed non-state soldiers, and

---

[5] In the 2011 census, the Dalit were 16.6% of the population, or about 200 million.
[6] The British were pioneers when they encouraged the creation of affirmative action-type programs for the Dalit in the early 1900s.

intergenerational bonded laborers where children inherited the debts of their parents. Most slaves were Dalit.

The importance Hindus place on caste hierarchy is known and culturally ingrained. [cxxvii] It was not going to be modified with unenforced national laws, no matter how many were passed. As previously noted by American law professor Mark Movsesian, "law that does not reflect the values of a society is bound to fail."

Social castes are not limited to India or Hinduism. In this region, Muslims in India, Pakistan, and Bangladesh observe a caste system. So do Buddhists in Sri Lanka. Like India, some have laws that prevent discrimination by caste, but if people see castes as ordinary and not discriminatory, there is nothing to enforce or prevent.

Muslims in India face discrimination and it can be severe. Nearly 200 million strong (14.2% of the population), Muslims face discrimination that affects many aspects of life, like where they live and work, their education, and their status in society.[cxxviii] Discrimination recently became more severe. A 2019 citizenship law uses religion to decide which legal refugees can become citizens. Muslims cannot. In combination with a citizenship verification process and a national registry for citizens, many multi-generational resident Muslims fear they could lose their rights as citizens. These actions are unsettling for Muslims, and that appears to be intentional. [cxxix] Then again, India, the world's most populous socialist *democracy,* ironically has many discriminatory laws that affect non-Hindus. [cxxx]

Discrimination is a real problem in this region, and it has gotten worse since independence. Some of it is legal, some illegal, conscious and unconscious, and almost all has ties to religion. The King of Bhutan saw diversity as an unaffordable luxury that creates problems for social harmony and unity. The actions of many in this region indicate agreement, although it may not be seen as a desirable luxury. Is discrimination seen as a major problem? Of thirteen domestic issues, in 2018 Indians placed communal relations as the least important.[cxxxi]

## European Overseas Empires – New World

For Europe's empires, the New World represented three continents of lucrative economic opportunities, with grossly insufficient labor to capitalize on them. The empires had some answers for insufficient labor. Europe had many unwelcome and unwanted people, and insufficient opportunities that left people in poverty. These people could voluntarily or involuntarily emigrate. So could people that wanted to try to fulfill the dream of a better life but had no chance because they were born into the wrong class or lacked connections. They also had a nascent slave trade with plenty of room to grow. In the 19th century, there was also colonial labor that needed work.

Over the centuries, immigrants voluntarily and involuntarily came to the New World from every Old-World continent to fill labor needs. Skilled labor came from Europe, and unskilled labor initially came from the most cost-effective sources. Over time laws on human rights evolved, slavery and indentured servitude were abolished, skill requirements changed, and there were concerns about the size of some minority populations. All of this influenced the selection of labor sources, deprioritized cost as the primary determinant, and motivated a shift toward recruiting immigrants from Europe.

In Europe's overseas colonies in the Americas, labor needs in the 16th through early 20th centuries were met by prisoners from the motherlands, indigenous populations, slaves primarily from Africa, indentured servants from Asia and Europe, and voluntary immigrants from Europe. The two New World America continents became diverse composites of indigenous people from, or descended from, Old World Africa, Asia, and Europe. New World Oceania wasn't colonized until the mid-18th century. Extra needs for labor were mostly fulfilled by indigenous populations, and voluntary and involuntary immigrants from different countries in Europe, Asia, and Oceania. On all three New World continents, discrimination followed diversity.

## Latam – Pre-1945

The first and primary colonizers of Latin America (Latam) were the Spanish and Portuguese in the late 15th and early 16th centuries. Tales of gold and silver brought scores of settlers and immigrants from the Iberian Peninsula, and smaller populations from other European countries. They came to get rich and initially did it on the backs of the indigenous people, collectively called the Amerindians. If the backbreaking labor didn't kill them, diseases of the white man did because they had no natural immunities to the imported diseases of smallpox, diphtheria, typhus, and influenza. Estimates for the Amerindian population in 1500 vary, with 50 million as a middle estimate.[77] One hundred years later the Amerindian population was up to 95% smaller.[cxxxii] People of European blood were the new majority.

Opportunities to mine gold and silver, and grow sugar, indigo, and cocoa required additional labor. The Portuguese had a solution. They had trading posts in their west African colonies that were already selling slaves to Europe. In 1526 the Atlantic slave trade began. In time other European empires participated as buyers, transporters, and sellers.[78] Portugal remained the most significant player, delivering an estimated 5.8 million slaves and most to its Brazilian colony.

Latam buyers purchased about 95% of the estimated 10–13 million Africans sold in the Atlantic slave trade. About half worked the plantations on islands in the Caribbean.[79] The demand for slaves throughout the New World Americas (Latam and English-speaking North America (ESNA)) was mostly for men, because plantations and mining required heavy lifting. On a total of 630 slave ships to the Americas, 46% of the slaves were men, and 26% each for women and children. [cxxxiii]

"The relationship between African and New World slavery was highly complementary. African slave owners demanded primarily women and

---

[77] Estimates range from 10–100 million.

[78] After 1776 the US participated and American enterprises, mostly from Rhode Island and South Carolina, transported about 1% of the slaves in this trade. In 1808 it became a crime in the US to import or export slaves.

[79] Some smaller colonies in the Caribbean became part of ESNA when the Spanish Empire lost them to the British Empire and they became English speaking.

children for labour and lineage incorporation and tended to kill males because they were troublesome and likely to flee. The transatlantic trade, on the other hand, demanded primarily adult males for labour and thus saved from certain death many adult males who otherwise would have been slaughtered outright by their African captors." [cxxxiv]

Brazil was the largest procurer of slaves and in 1888 it became the last New World nation to abolish slavery. (Cuba was second to last, with abolition in 1886.) When it did, it had a majority population that was black and mulatto. In other parts of Latam, and most saliently Peru, forced labor or outright slavery of Pacific islanders persisted until around 1890.

Societies in Latam were ordered with a system called the *casta*. A person's status was based on blood purity. People born in Spain or Portugal, (actually any Christian born in Europe) that was 100% white, and was not a crypto-Catholic,[80] was deemed to have the purest blood. Called the *Peninsulares*, they sat at the top of the casta. Next up were criollos or creoles, the Peninsulares Latam-born children. Peninsulares and creoles were the largest landholders, and they controlled the governments and economies. Amerindians were supposed to be considered one of the pure races. Reality told a story of blood purity being white blood.

Maintaining blood purity was essential to retain a position at the top of the hierarchy. It might seem simple to do this at a time when miscegenation was either illegal or socially taboo throughout the world, but in Latam white males outnumbered white females and miscegenation was condoned. It was common for black and Amerindian females to voluntarily or forcibly become companions. There was a significant benefit to having a child that was mulatto or mestizo. These were the brown people, and they formed the next level in the casta.[81] Below this were people who had not a trace of white blood. First came free blacks and zambos, a black and Amerindian mix.[82] At the very bottom of the casta were slaves. Most were black, but some were Amerindian.[83, cxxxv]

**Latam independence.** In 1804, free and enslaved blacks in Haiti completed a successful revolution against France, led by Napoleon Bonaparte, to become the first nation in Latam to gain independence. Napoleon had wanted to keep Haiti to maintain revenue from sugar to finance wars in Europe. The Haitians weren't cooperating. Free and enslaved blacks and mulattoes were 90% of Haiti's population and they wanted an end to their brutal French slave masters. Half of Haiti's slaves died after a few years of labor.[cxxxvi] Motivations for independence increased in 1802 when Haitians learned that France revoked the abolishment of slavery, and they became victims of one of the earliest documented cases of genocide. Napoleon ordered the killing of all blacks over twelve.[cxxxvii] Shortly after independence the

---

[80] Crypto-Catholics were Muslims or Jews that converted to Catholicism during the Spanish Inquisition but continued to hold the beliefs of Islam or Judaism respectively.

[81] In Brazil, brown people are called *pardos*.

[82] There were many more categories of mixed persons.

[83] Amerindians that converted to Christianity were supposed to be protected subjects. To discourage Amerindian enslavement, in the 16th century the Catholic Church forbade the mistreatment or unjust enslavement of Amerindians. It was not very effective. Neither was the Spanish Crown's bans on the slavery of Amerindians in 1493 and 1530.

Haitians ordered the killing of all European-born French. An estimated 20,000 were slaughtered in the 1804 Haitian Massacre.[cxxxviii] Haiti's population was now virtually all black and mulatto.

At independence, there was a belief that anyone with black ancestry would have the same social status, but this was mistaken. In colonial Haiti, some mulattoes were permitted to buy or inherit the land of their white fathers. At independence, mulattoes had economic power, but the blacks did not. They also had lighter skin, which continued to infer superiority. Mulattoes became a superior class; at least until a black became the leader of Haiti. Rotating discrimination between blacks and mulattoes tied to the national leader's ancestry became a staple of Haitian society.[cxxxix] Something similar has occurred in Trinidad and Tobago. African-Trinidadians are descendants of slaves and Indo-Trinidadians are descendants of indentured servants. Each represents about 40% of the population. Discrimination, or at least perceptions of discrimination, rise and fall depending on the national leader's ancestry. Indo-Trinidadians perceive more discrimination when the national leader is African-Trinidadian and vice versa.

Most Latam colonies became independent in the early 19th century (1810-1828). On the practice of slavery, independent Latam was very different from colonial Latam. Decisions to abolish slavery took shape during preparations for the wars for independence. Slaves and free blacks agreed to fight for the side that offered the greatest freedoms. Blacks would be key to the Colonials winning independence. However, freedom was often not immediate. It would take until the mid 1850s for most nations in this region to abolish slavery.

Abolishing slavery created the need for a new labor source. Hundreds of thousands of indentured servants, mostly from European colonies in Asia, made the long journey to the New World. The British recruited from the Indian sub-continent, the Dutch from Indonesia, and Spain from the Philippines. Some were also kidnapped. In today's parlance, they were victims of human trafficking. People in need of work from Japan and China also became indentured servants. Indentured servants brought ethnic but also religious diversity to the overwhelmingly Roman Catholic Latam because most followed Hinduism, Islam, or eastern religions.[84,cxl]

Blacks enjoyed a period of heightened social status as free enfranchised citizens. Elections brought many black and mulatto politicians into office. Mexico's president, Vincente Guerrero (April 1829 to December 1829) wasn't elected; he came to office in a coup. He was of mixed Amerindian and African descent. Armed with national power he abolished slavery and became an advocate for social justice. Some feared Guerrero would lead the majority Amerindians to marginalize the whites. Less than a year after assuming office, he was ejected in a coup and killed by a firing squad in 1931.

Guerrero as an Amerindian was unhappy about European conquest and rule, and like many people with African ancestry, he was angry about slavery. For whites, the possibility of blacks seeking revenge conjured up images of the Haitian Massacre (1804). This possibility seemed very real. In some nations, the abolishment of slavery led to whites losing their free-men majority. In others there was concern that

---

[84] Indentured servants commonly worked plantations in Brazil, Guyana, Peru, Suriname, and some Caribbean states.

they could lose it. Whites continued to enjoy economic power, and they used that to regain political control. Measures were taken to solidify white majorities. Latam went through a whitening period. In the first 100 years of independence 6–11 million mostly southern Europeans migrated to different Latam countries. But more were wanted. Several nations including Argentina, Brazil, Chile, Uruguay, and Costa Rica secured white majorities, but some that wanted them did not.[85,cxli]

Not having a white majority did not mean whites could not control government. New legislation restricted voting to men with certain levels of education and land ownership. This hit blacks hard, but men of all colors were affected. The voting population was reduced to percentages that were often under 5-10%. (Some nations kept restrictions into the 1980s.[86])

With whites back in control, marginalization returned to black and mixed-race populations. It wasn't long before the *casta* system was reimplemented with tweaks.[87] Discriminatory practices in independent Latam were looking a lot like those from the ruling periods of the Spanish and Portuguese empires.

Latam was the New World region with the largest indigenous population. It was the recipient of the largest number of African slaves, and second to English Speaking North America (ESNA) for the arrival of European settlers and immigrants. Uniquely, it became a region where racial mixing was ordinary among whites, blacks, and Amerindians. There is no other region that comes close to having a diverse mix of people with African, Asian, European, American, and mixed blood. This might seem like a great composition for people to naturally dispense with discrimination, but this has not been the case.

## Racism and anti-Racism in Latam after 1945
(See Appendix for list of countries)

After WWII there was a good deal of soul searching on discriminatory practices in the New World, but this did not include Latam. How could national leaders in some of Latam's largest countries (Argentina, Brazil, and Chile) provide a safe haven for Nazi war criminals and be compelled to soul search on Nazi-initiated genocides? Then again, governments in Latam were not democratic. Most were original signatories of the UN Charter, but like so many other nations they did not take seriously their commitment to equal fundamental freedoms for all. Fifty years later, things were different. By 1995 almost all countries had transitioned toward democracy with enumerated freedoms. Disenfranchisement policies ended, some non-white national leaders were elected, and some anti-discrimination laws were passed.

---

[85] Latam was competing for immigrants with the United States, but it was not as attractive, and people in Europe knew it. Most European immigrants to Latam had been landless peasants anxious to escape poverty and continuous wars in Europe. Reports to relatives back home described fewer wars, but also few opportunities to secure land or become rich.

[86] Because Latam has a long and enduring history of dictatorships, voting rights were often inconsequential because votes were absent or symbolic.

[87] Tweaks were needed because it had become difficult to identify who was mixed with black, white, or indigenous blood.

Anti-discrimination legislation is step one. Amerindians are seen as having a legitimate claim as original inhabitants and landowners, and they are readily accepted as needing anti-discrimination laws. This is not always true for blacks. Blacks in some nations have only recently been granted or they still lack equal constitutional rights, and they do not have the protection of anti-discrimination laws.[cxlii] Where laws have been passed, enforcement is step two, and this has sputtered, particularly for blacks.

Compared to whites, Amerindians and blacks in Latam have far greater rates of poverty and they often lack access to basic services like potable water and electricity. Violence against blacks can be horrid because it can be condoned or legally perpetrated by police. In Ecuador, the targeting of blacks by police is a formal part of their jobs. The police "conceive of their mission as protecting citizens from the danger' of blacks. These blacks are not viewed as citizens but rather as violent intruders that invade the cities."[cxliii,88] In other nations, blacks believe the police think it is their job to physically mistreat them. [cxliv] Blacks, in addition to gypsies, Asians and Arabs were legally prohibited from immigrating to El Salvador from 1933 to the 1980s.

Data like this is not a deterrent to fervent denials that racism exists;[cxlv,cxlvi] at least, some rationalize, not in the form present in other countries, like the United States.[cxlvii] Denial is supported by the lack of a formal casta (social hierarchy), as if discrimination must be enshrined in law to count, and also by framing discrimination against blacks as not based on race but rather socio-economic status. This makes it not racism. [cxlviii] But racial discrimination against blacks and Amerindians is plainly evident.[cxlix]

The greater attention to anti-discrimination legislation and enforcement can't be too effective for the Amerindians. Amerindians continue to face land confiscations without compensation, limited rights over land, and exclusion from discussions about land even when guaranteed by the constitution.[cl,cli] In a 2005 report, the latest available from the International Labor Office (ILO), it was estimated that there were 1.3 million forced laborers in Latam, of which "substantial numbers" were Amerindians.[clii] According to the UN, discrimination against Amerindians remains a problem. Forced labor would support this. Blatant discrimination occurs even in the fourteen countries where Amerindians and mestizos are a majority or a significant minority (>25<50%).[cliii] Ironically these are most of the same countries that created multicultural constitutions between 1985 and 2000. The objective was to give Amerindians control over their "nations."[89] These initiatives have been lauded as progressive forms of democracy. The problem with the applause is that there have been outcomes familiar to most multicultural initiatives. Amerindians may be more comfortable in their nations, but segregation encourages discrimination, which can be blatant and severe, and it leads to fewer economic opportunities. Has this contributed to receptivity to forced labor?

---

[88] In the 19th century nascent American police forces targeted "dangerous classes." These were blacks, foreign immigrants (mostly Irish and Italian), and the poor.
[89] In Guatemala the motivation may have been the massacres and genocide of Mayan Amerindians between 1981 and 1983.

Do Latin Americans see discrimination and marginalization of Amerindians and blacks as major problems? Generally, no. Denials of racism would prevent this. From time-to-time populist/socialist politicians promising to end social injustice and inequality are elected. The platforms of Latam's populists have the sound of modern-day Robin Hoods stealing from the wealthy oligarchs and foreign corporations and giving to the poor black and Amerindian masses.[90] These messages get people elected, even though time and again Latam populism/socialism leads to high inflation, and even hyperinflation, increased corruption, higher crime, lowered real wages, and increased political instability.[cliv] Populists have set economic development back in Argentina, Brazil, Chile, Peru, Mexico, Nicaragua, and Venezuela. The people hurt the most are the very people it was supposed to help. [clv]

Overall, blacks and mulattoes represent 25% of Latam's population, or about 150 million. A combined black and mulatto population is a majority in Brazil, the Dominican Republic, and Haiti. In Haiti, blacks and mulattoes are an overwhelming majority, but as noted above this is not a homogenous majority. In the Dominican Republic mulattoes and blacks are an overwhelming majority, but blacks face severe discrimination. Under the military dictatorship of Rafael Trujillo (1933-1961) people were forbidden from identifying as black or mulatto on national identity cards: the options were white or indigenous. Later options included indio, a black and white mix. Because African ancestry is undesirable, almost all Dominicans lessen this by identifying as indio. An indio identity, however, doesn't prevent discrimination if someone has darker skin. People with darker skin can be confused with the despised Haitians who share the island of Hispaniola. In 2010, the Dominican constitution was altered. People born in the Dominican Republic were automatically citizens, but they had to be able to prove they were born there. Many ethnic Haitians born in the Dominican Republic lacked birth certificates, and 70-80,000 were deported.[clvi]

In the United States comparisons have been done with Brazilian blacks that find Brazil providing a favorable and less discriminatory environment. Blacks in Brazil would disagree. To this day, the disparities between blacks and mulattoes, and whites, is called social apartheid. In 2019 Brazil had a majority black and mulatto population. In the United States the black population was 13.4%. In 2018 Brazilian blacks and mulattos earned 26% of whites. In the United States it was 78%.[clvii] In the late 20th century Brazil used separate service entrances for blacks.[clviii] In 2020 a black Brazilian was 15 times more likely to be killed by a police officer than an African-American.[clix] In 2016 the United States had a black president, and Brazil had no black cabinet members. In the last three Brazilian presidential administrations, there has been a total of one black cabinet member. "We black Brazilians don't blame our national black leaders for inefficiency or inaccuracy because we don't have any." [clx] Neither did blacks in South Africa's apartheid.

Slavery, indentured servitude, immigration, indigenous populations, and miscegenation turned Latam into the world's most racially and ethnically diverse region in the world. An estimated 40% of the region's population is mixed race. It seems improbable that there can be blatant discrimination against blacks, mulattoes, Amerindians, zambos, or mestizos but there is. Maybe it's because racism isn't really

[90] Populism is sometimes equated to politicians that pander to the concerns of the masses to improve popularity; this is not the populism of Latam.

addressed because it's generally not seen as a problem. The non-problem may be getting worse. Latam-style populism with a history of leaving minorities worse off has increased "socio-economic" discrimination. But then again this is not racial discrimination or illegal.


# Oceania – Pre-1945

Europeans began settling Oceania 2.5 centuries after Latam, and slave labor was no longer an option, unless it was prison labor. Between 1788 and 1868 162,000 convicts from Britain (includes Ireland) were transported to Australia and hired out as indentured labor. Prisoners became Australian settlers. Their crimes were often trivial, including stealing chickens, sheep, handkerchiefs, potatoes or cheese. Indentured servants treated more like slaves could also be members of indigenous populations. Australia has two small populations of indigenous dark-skinned people called Aboriginals and Torres Straight Islanders.[clxi] New Zealand has a larger indigenous population called Maoris. They were not enslaved, but they did enslave; mostly people captured in wars. [clxii] Maori slavery continued into the 1860s.

Indigenous populations could not satisfy all the needs for labor and neither could convicts, particularly because the practice of transporting convicts was temporary. Small populations of indentured servants from India, China and larger populations from nearby Pacific islands voluntarily or forcibly came to work in Australia (and also New Zealand). Blackbirding was a term applied to the coercion of Pacific Islanders, to work as unpaid or poorly paid laborers in Australia and New Zealand.[clxiii, 91] However, the primary labor source for Australia and New Zealand were immigrants from Northern Europe. Most immigrants went to Australia, the giant of Oceania.

At first discrimination fell on the indigenous and the convicts; the latter with an emphasis on the Irish Catholics. With increasing diversity came ethnic discrimination. In 1901 Australia became virtually independent from Britain, and one of its earliest actions was to implement the "White Australia" immigration policy. It effectively banned immigrants from Asia and the Pacific islands, called for the deportation of existing non-white contract laborers, and denied citizenship to Asians, Africans, and the indigenous populations. It also effectively banned whites from the south and east of Europe. More appropriate nicknames for this policy would have been Australia's Northern White European immigration policy, Diversity Reversal, or Homogeneity Redux. New Zealand's immigration policy, which restricted Asian immigrants, was comparatively liberal.

In 1945 Australia's population was again homogenous—definitely white, predominantly Christian, English-speaking and of northern European blood. The small indigenous populations in Australia continued to face severe discrimination. Discrimination against New Zealand's Maori was less in part because most had assimilated by adopting Christianity and the English language. Among the other

---

[91] Several Pacific island nations and some in Latam also purchased labor from the Blackbirds. The practice was made illegal in 1890.

island nations in Oceania, racial discrimination was tempered by homogenous populations. Fiji with its large population of indentured servants from India was an exception.

Oceania's experiences with diversity and discrimination are in some ways similar to other New World regions. These were all lands that attracted diverse people in search of better economic opportunities, and early on leveraged forced labor to maximize production. When the population became too diverse, there were whitening periods and policies, although the "White Australia" policy was the most extreme.

## Oceania - Racism and anti-Racism after 1945
### (See Appendix for list of countries)

In 1945, Australia and New Zealand committed to delivering equal fundamental freedoms for all. Since then, they have taken many measures to make good on this commitment. In 1975 and 1993 Australia and New Zealand respectively passed laws to protect people from racial discrimination and implemented immigration policies that did not discriminate on race, ethnicity, or religion. Immigrants began arriving from Asia, Africa, and Central and Eastern Europe. They were Buddhist, Christian, Hindu, and Muslim. In a relatively brief period of time, Australia's non-white and indigenous population rose to 24%.

This dramatic influx of diversity in a condensed period of time has noticeably increased discrimination. More than half of Australians view African- and Muslim-Australians unfavorably. Conscious or unconscious biases would naturally be very high. [clxiv] It is natural for people that perceive discrimination to return the biased favor. A 2019 study among school children by Australian National University and Western Sydney University found white children saying they experienced discrimination half as much as those from minorities.

Discrimination against the indigenous populations has nothing to do with recency; they arrived 50-70,000 years ago. In 1962 the Australian government granted them the right to vote. Also, in the 1960s the Aborigines organized a civil rights movement to motivate an end to discrimination.[92] By 1972, the government agreed that integration was not lessening discrimination and agreed to a multicultural arrangement with the Aborigines that included self-government. In 1999, the policy was deemed a failure and abolished. Self-government remained subsidized. The rationale was tied up in payments for historical sins. Australians were also meant to issue an apology. The actions of the white Australians were being compared to the Nazis and the Holocaust. It's not a secret that calling people and their ancestors, in this case the majority race, horrific names is more likely to increase bias than encourage contrition.[93]

Some of the arguments against this subsidized multicultural arrangement are familiar.

---

[92] From 1960 to 1969, aboriginal children were taken from their homes to work as domestic servants as part of the Aborigines Protection Act.

[93] The Australians played a key role in ending WWII. Being called a Nazi would really sting.

"We are dealing with collective self-accusation, complicated by the fact that the hands that beat the breast are not the hands that committed the offence.

Certainly, it is the case that saturating indigenous peoples in a mist of self-referential Western sympathy is merely one [benevolently racist] way in which *we* use *them* for the luxury of our own self-regard." Kenneth Minogue, London School of Economics, 1998.

Widespread sympathy was not enough to alter the conclusion that Australia's Aborigines had to join the mainstream with other Australians. The government believed it made no sense to permit the Aborigines to live as "hunter-gatherers" and have their lives made comfortable by the transfer of billions of dollars. [clxv]

Indigenous populations have received other attention and support. In 1993 the Native Title Act was passed. This overturned a British claim that Australia was *terra nullius* (nobody's land). This allowed the Aboriginals to make claims for land compensation. These claims have dragged on in the courts, many for decades. In 2019 an award of $1.78 million gave hope that many other indigenous people would be compensated for land claims.

The slow pace of integration among indigenous populations continues to drive discrimination. In the Australian Government's Health Performance Framework 2014 Report, they indicated that discrimination against Aboriginals is still considered by many as ordinary.

Compensation for land to the Maori of New Zealand was more in line with the process in the United States. Some land had been lost in wars, in this case wars fought over land (with compensation often but now always following). The sale of most land was, however, negotiated. By 1910, the Maori had relinquished title to 99% of the south island and 75% of the north island. However, after the fact, some Maori felt they had been pressured to accept a crummy offer. In 1998 New Zealand paid an additional $170 million to the Maori for land claims.

New Zealand was ahead of other nations in granting the right to vote in 1867 to all Maori males. This was twelve years before all white males. It was also first to give women the right to vote in 1893. New Zealand with a population of just 5 million, is often held up for the progress it has made addressing discrimination. In 2015, Martin Prosperity Institute gave it an award for being the most racially and ethnically tolerant country. This may reflect New Zealand's newer leniency toward multiculturalism, and special bicultural attention for its large Maori population (15%). The Maori do not see themselves or their issues as one with non-indigenous minorities. New Zealand's shift toward multiculturalism has had failures similar to other implementations. It has reified differences, making them more concrete, and inspiring unconscious discrimination. It has also been criticized for being race based and discriminatory against non-Maori minorities.[clxvi]

At independence in 1970, Fiji's population was half indigenous Fijians and half Indo-Fijians. The latter are mostly descendants of Hindu and some Muslim Indian indentured servants and free laborers that arrived in Fiji between 1870 and 1920 to work Fiji's sugar plantations. Fiji's constitution placed limits on Indo-Fijian land ownership that has created a two-tiered society. The indigenous Fijians are the landowners, and the Indo-Fijians are the leaseholders. When leases expire many have not been renewed and Indo-Fijians who have worked the land for generations have had few options to survive beyond emigrating.[clxvii] According to the Fijian census in 2004 Indo-Fijians were about 38% of the population. Present on the island for more than 100 years, Indo-Fijians face legal and rampant discrimination that has encouraged many to emigrate and start over.

Australia and New Zealand have developed a multiple decade track record of significantly increasing diversity and trying to simultaneously address discrimination. Discrimination in employment, education, and some other areas is not legal. What specifically constitutes discrimination, proof of discrimination, and the remedies for violators are a work in process. This makes sense because increased levels of diversity and discrimination are quite new. One thing is known. It was much easier to increase diversity and to legally provide for fundamental freedoms for all, than it has been to create nations where diverse people do not regularly consciously or unconsciously discriminate.

# United States and Canada - Pre-1945

The colonization of ESNA by the British and French began in the early 17th century, trailing Latam by about a century. Like other New World colonies, economic opportunities exceeded the availability of labor. There were indigenous populations, called Native Americans in the future United States, and Native Canadians (or First Nations) in the future Canada. These populations were far fewer in number than Amerindians in Latam and they would have been insufficient for labor needs if they were amenable to the arrangements, and often they were not. Labor needs were primarily satisfied with indentured servants from Europe and Asia, black slaves, European settlers and immigrants, and offspring of all the above. Fulfilling labor needs created unprecedented levels of diversity. Discrimination followed. [94,95,96]

British prisoners represented about 10-17% (about 60–70,000 to 100,000 - 128,000) of the European settlers to the Thirteen Colonies. [97, clxviii] British prisoners continued to be transported here until the end of the Revolutionary War. Many were sold as slaves, although their identity as convicts was withheld.[98,clxix] Many were political prisoners and commonly Irish Catholics.[99] Some, mostly Scots, were prisoners of war. Most others committed what today would be considered

---

[94] Some indentured servants from Europe were enslaved and others lived in slave-like conditions into the 20th century.

[95] Early on several thousand Native Americans were enslaved as spoils of war. In 1750 Native American-chattel slavery officially ended, but forced and bonded labor persisted.

[96] Native-Americans and Native-Canadians also enslaved conquered indigenous tribes.

[97] Settlers are distinguished from immigrants because they arrived earlier and helped to build the early settlements in the colonies.

[98] During the American Revolutionary War (1775-1783), instead of British prisoners being enslaved in the Thirteen Colonies; they became belligerent soldiers.

[99] For some time in the 17th century, the colony of Massachusetts forbade the import of Irish "servants."

misdemeanors, such as stealing food. This is one reason it has been said, with great exaggeration, that a bunch of chicken thieves settled America. Chicken thieves were a minority of the country's settlers, but criminals, often petty thieves, and other wrongdoers were numerous. The British viewed some northern colonies as places to "drain away their filth."[clxx]

The first indentured servants were European. Many were fleeing religious persecution and poverty, and most came from the British Isles. An estimated 50–70% of the *settlers* to the Thirteen Colonies (about 300,000– 375,000) couldn't afford their passage so they exchanged servitude for transport.[100] Servitude in exchange for the chance to practice their religion, have better economic opportunities, and the possibility of land ownership were considered a good trade. The average age was between fourteen and sixteen, and most were under nineteen.[clxxi] Some were kidnapped, and others legally sent by their parents or the state. Sending children to the colonies was a solution to pauper children on the streets of Britain. Indentured servants served 4–20-year contracts.[101] Most never experienced better economic opportunities or land ownership, only hard labor, and for many female servants, sexual abuse. Only 40% outlasted their contracts. For the other 60% indentured servitude was not temporary; it was analogous to slavery. Survivors received "freedom dues," which could include food, clothes, a gun and even land. Early on some were granted plots of land that could be 10 hectares (25 acres) or more.[clxxii]

Early on blacks were indentured servants with defined terms, much like their white counterparts. Black and white servants worked side by side and were treated equally, including eligibility for freedom dues. In the mid-17th century former indentured servants were gaining a reputation as troublemakers. This was added to the complaint that it was expensive to train and retrain new servants. These views were especially applicable to the Irish Catholics despised for their religion and ignorance. The hatred of Catholics had travelled from Britain to the Thirteen Colonies.

The perceived failures of indentured servitude in the mid- to late-17th century instigated the use of slavery as a preferred labor source and blacks became chattel slaves. The colonials might have liked to make the Irish Catholics chattel slaves, but at this time, slaves were non-Christians. Later the slave designation changed to be defined by race rather than religion.[clxxiii, clxxiv] As chattel slaves, blacks and their offspring became the permanent property of their masters with limited opportunities for manumission. Between the arrival of the first slaves in 1619 and the end of the trade in 1808[102] an estimated 388,000 black slaves landed in the United States.[clxxv]

The population of Native Canadians was quite small, spread out,[103] and insufficient for labor needs. Needs were far less than the United States with its more

---

[100] Virginia and Maryland had an abundance of economic opportunities. Plantation owners were rewarded with 50 acres of land for each indentured servant they brought to their colonies.

[101] According to emmigationinfo.com about 300,000 indentured servants were Irish, and their contracts were for periods of 7–20 years. The contract for British servants was 4–7 years.

[102] Purchasing slaves became illegal on January 1, 1808. Discussions about ending the slave trade and the Louisiana Purchase ignited sales. About 25 % of all slaves purchased in the United States took place between 1801 and 1807.

[103] In the 17th century, according to Canada's Commission on Aboriginal Health the indigenous population of the land that would ultimately form the borders of an independent Canada's was about

temperate climate and plantations. Plantations were the grandest driver of slavery. Still slavery was not uncommon. Most slaves were Native Canadians working on the lands of Native Canadians where slavery was an ordinary practice following conquests. Slave owning by Canadian colonists was considered widespread because many people owned a small number of slaves. Some had been gifts from Native Canadians, of which some were black. Prior to America's Revolutionary War, slaves were twice as likely to be Native Canadians as blacks. After the War, American Loyalists that were slaveowners were allowed to bring to Canada "negros [sic], household furniture, utensils of husbandry, or cloathing [sic]" duty-free." None could be sold for at least a year. Now indigenous and black slaves were similar in number and estimated in total at about 8,000. Slavery was abolished throughout the British Empire, of which Canada was part, in 1834.[clxxvi]

Native Americans also practiced slavery, including the enslavement of African Americans. "The Five Civilized Tribes [Cherokee, Choctaw, Chickasaw, Creek, and Seminole] were deeply committed to slavery, established their own racialized black codes, immediately reestablished slavery when they arrived in Indian territory, rebuilt their nations with slave labor [when relocating west of the Mississippi], crushed slave rebellions, and enthusiastically sided with the Confederacy in the Civil War."[clxxvii,clxxviii]

The grandest presence of slavery in ESNA was in Europe's plantation-filled colonies in the Caribbean. These colonies qualified as slave economies with black to white ratios ranging from 4:1 to 10:1.

At independence in 1776, the population of the United States was 2.5 million. The majority had English blood, with significant Irish, Scottish, and German minorities. Blacks were about 17% of the population, and most were slaves (92%).[104] The population of free blacks increased significantly after independence.[105] Americans in the north became conscious of the hypocrisy of claiming natural human rights, while at the same time denying them to Africans.[clxxix] By 1804 all northern states had abolished slavery, and slavery was forbidden in the Northwest Territories. But being free and being equal were two different concepts. Black Codes made some states unwelcoming to free blacks.

In the south, slavery remained legal. Some southern slaves were freed and some purchased slaves, some as wives, but also to give them a better life.[106] A smaller number ran plantations with significant slave populations.[clxxx,clxxxi]

In 1822, the American Colonization Society purchased land in the future nation of Liberia in Africa to create a new home for free blacks. This was one of several Back to Africa initiatives. Some were led by whites and others by blacks. All had a similar

---

500,000.

[104] In 1776 less than 150,000 slaves had arrived in the Thirteen Colonies. A population of 400,000 reflects procreation.

[105] Immediately after independence, black loyalists (about 4,000) were granted their freedom by the British and transported to Nova Scotia. Discrimination led many to be transported to London. Here they became the Black Poor of London. Many were then transported to Britain's colony in Sierra Leone, where many were sold to white settlers as apprentices.

[106] In most of the south, a purchased slave by anyone remained a slave because manumission was illegal.

rationale; blacks could not escape discrimination or a history of slavery in the United States. At least not for a while. Estimates to equality were more than 250 years.[107]

In the early 1800s, labor needs would continue to grow because the US was expanding westward. The United States believed it had a manifest destiny to expand its borders from the Atlantic Ocean to the Pacific Ocean and south to the Caribbean Sea and Gulf of Mexico. This destiny was complicated by the long-time residents and owners of this land: the Native Americans, the British in the pacific northwest, and the Spanish in the southwest.[108] Obtaining land from the latter two was accomplished by wars and treaties. The former was more complicated. The history between the Native Americans and colonials and later Americans included collaboration and conflict over land, including some very serious wars where Native Americans allied with the British or French to defend or increase their land. Native Americans sided with the French in the French and Indian Wars (1754-1763). The French conceded quite a bit of land that was coveted or settled by Native Americans in North America to the British and Spanish. Most Native American tribes fought with the British and against the Americans in the Revolutionary War and the War of 1812.[109] Native Americans lost millions of acres of land in treaties the British negotiated with the Americans when ending these wars. Land (and many lives) was also lost in other American-Indian wars.

In an independent United States, provisions were made with the Native Americans for consents, treaties and compensation for land. Dozens of signed treaties exchanged land for some combination of new land, services and monetary compensation.

"In the end, the story of the colonization of the United States is still a story of power, but it was a more subtle and complex kind of power than we conventionally recognize. It was the power to establish the legal institutions and the rules by which land transactions would be enforced. The threat of physical force would always be present, but most of the time it could be kept out of view because it was not needed. Anglo-Americans could sincerely believe, for most of American history, that they were not conquerors, because they believed they were buying land from the Indians in the same way they bought land from each other. What kind of conqueror takes such care to draft contracts to keep up the appearance that no conquest is taking place? A conqueror that genuinely does not think of itself as one."[clxxxii]

Stuart Banner, UCLA School of Law

Canada also fought many wars with Native Canadians during its westward expansion, and it too leveraged treaties to secure land. Like the United States resistance resulted in some forced relocations that would later be solidified in treaties.[110]

---

[107] The 2020 estimate for gender equality is 208 years.

[108] Native Americans dispute British and Spanish ownership, but at this time these were considered the "lawful" owners.

[109] A few Indian tribes allied with the Americans. Most allied with the British and Canada. Two major outcomes: Native Americans lost their land in more than six states, and they lost their British ally.

Wars and land negotiations with the Native Americans took place in an environment where the United States population was soaring. By 1870 the US population was 15 times larger than in 1776. About one-third of the newest immigrants were German. One third came from northern Europe excluding the Irish, who independently represented a third. A letter to the London Times from an Irish immigrant in 1850 illustrated why immigrants were flocking to the United States. "I am exceedingly well pleased at coming to this land of plenty. On arrival I purchased 120 acres of land at $5 an acre. You must bear in mind that I have purchased the land out, and it is to me and mine an 'estate forever,' without a landlord, an agent or tax-gatherer to trouble me. I would advise all my friends to quit Ireland — the country most dear to me; as long as they remain in it, they will be in bondage and misery."[clxxxiii]

Amazing about this sentiment in 1850 is that discrimination against the Irish was pervasive, but it was much less than what they faced at home under British rule. "In the popular press, the Irish were depicted as subhuman. They were carriers of disease. They were drawn as lazy, clannish, unclean, drunken brawlers who wallowed in crime and bred like rats. In 1849 the secret Order of the Star-Spangled Banner was founded in New York to resist Catholic immigration. The Protestants wanted to stop the growth of the Irish minority."[clxxxiv]

Just before the Civil War began, with the exception of about thirty-five black slaves in twenty-five northern states, blacks were free everywhere but the south. Almost all slaves in 1860 lived in the eleven southern states comprising the Confederacy. There were 250,000 free blacks and 3,951,000 slaves. Most slaves were in the deep south (70%).[clxxxv] The Confederacy was committed to maintaining the status quo of slavery. For the Union's twenty-five northern states the Confederacy's position put the United States of America at risk. The Union had the economic and population heft to end the possibility of the South's succession. It had double the population and the economy has been estimated as 4-10 times as large. The South had an agrarian economy, and the north was industrialized.[clxxxvi] America became the only nation in the world to fight a civil war to end slavery.

In 1863 the Emancipation Proclamation freed all of America's slaves. Radically, the United States also began using the word discrimination to acknowledge prejudiced behaviors. In the rest of the world, these behaviors were ordinary, and the United States was opening up a giant can of worms by acknowledging that some people faced discrimination. In 1866 the 14th Amendment to the US Constitution gave citizenship and the vote to male blacks and Native Americans that paid taxes. It also ended counting only 60% of slaves for purposes of apportioning legislative seats and determining federal taxation.

The three-fifths provision is often cited as a highly discriminatory law, but this fractional accounting did not impact the slaves, except in their favor. Slaves could not vote at this time, but slave masters could. More legislative power in the south was not a good omen for ending slavery or creating laws favorable to slaves. Fortunately, southern slave masters also didn't want to pay the same rate of taxation on slaves. They agreed to less tax for less representation and the Three-Fifths compromise.

[110] In British Colombia, CA land was declared terra nullius and remains unceded by the First Nations.

In 1870 the 15th Amendment offered a guarantee that the right to vote would not be denied "on account of race, color, or previous condition of servitude." The United States became a global leader in making the vote available to expanded populations and guaranteeing equal protection to all citizens under the law (Civil Rights Act of 1866). The attention given to emancipation and the right to vote gave rise to a new invigorated and unsuccessful movement for women to be emancipated and enfranchised.

From 1865 to 1877, the United States entered a period called Reconstruction where the government made efforts to remedy inequities with blacks. Under the Freedman's Bureau over 1,000 schools were built for blacks, investments were made in colleges, medical care, and the distribution of food. The Bureau may have had a longer life, but Andrew Johnson assumed the presidency after Lincoln was assassinated. He was a southerner and southern hostility to the Bureau made continuing services impossible. The Bureau was disbanded in 1872.

In some southern states, black voters outnumbered white voters. In 1868 the United States had its first black majority legislature in South Carolina. The notion of free slaves ruling whites set off alarms. Ex-confederate soldiers occupied many legislative and judicial positions in the south. They also founded the Ku Klux Clan in 1865. This influential combination was key to leveraging states' rights over voting. Laws were written to be colorblind and consistent with the US constitution and its new amendments, but disproportionately applied to blacks, (and Native Americans, and Irish Catholics). Objections to these measures were vigorous, but insufficient.[111]
Between 1870 and 1871 the United States passed three acts to protect the rights of African-Americans. This included the Civil Rights Act of 1871 which focused on extinguishing the Ku Klux Klan. The 1871 Act was successful, and the number of Klan members declined and then virtually disappeared, at least for a while. This became a familiar pattern. Laws were passed to protect civil rights for all, but workarounds surfaced. It was easy to do in a federal system where states' exercise considerable power.

With slavery ending, the United States looked for another source of inexpensive labor. It's hard to imagine that one year after abolishing slavery and involuntary servitude, US legislators passed the Immigration Act of 1864 permitting indentured servitude. Too poor to pay for their passage in advance, and not knowing the nightmare before them, southern Italians began flocking to America to work. Their working and living conditions were often very harsh and many were not free to leave their compounds until their debts were paid. Getting paid was not guaranteed. America had legitimized involuntary servitude the year after it was abolished. In 1874 Congress passed the Padrone Act. This was meant to end involuntary servitude, but workarounds allowed it to persist into the 1930s.[clxxxvii]

It wasn't the Ku Klux Clan but a mob in 1891 that perpetrated the largest mass lynching in the United States. Italians were victims. Formal policing in America was in nascent states, and police were more likely to do the bidding of politicians, wealthy businessmen and organized crime. For regular folk, vigilantes often carried out "justice." This hand of justice found more blacks than whites. Blacks were three

---

[111] The most vigorous opponents to the Jim Crow laws were white protestant Republicans and they could vote. That was a problem that the Klan addressed with intimidation tactics.

times more likely to be lynched than whites.[112,113] Lynching was a big problem and one that the president of the United States and many in Congress wanted to end. More than 200 bills were introduced in Congress to address lynching, but the southern states succeeded in stifling passage.

> All thoughtful men ... must feel the gravest alarm over the growth of lynching in this country, and especially over the peculiarly hideous forms so often taken by mob violence when colored men are the victims – on which occasions the mob seems to lay more weight, not on the crime but on the color of the criminal. ... There are certain hideous sights which when once seen can never be wholly erased from the mental retina...Whoever in any part of our country has ever taken part in lawlessly putting to death a criminal by the dreadful torture of fire must forever after have the awful spectacle of his own handiwork seared into his brain and soul. He can never again be the same man.
>
> President Theodore Roosevelt, 1903.

Opportunities in the United States continued to outpace the labor force. Western territories knee deep in the California gold rush found indentured laborers, most from China, as a solution. The Chinese quickly earned a reputation as very hard workers. In a nation that prized hard work that should have been a good thing, but they were rebranded as job stealers, and people that forced Americans to work for lower wages. In 1882 the United States passed the Chinese Exclusion Act, an immigration law that placed an ethnic/racial bias on immigrants. Like other nations, Americans wanted to minimize heterogeneity. White Americans preferred white immigrants—but not all whites.[114]

Similar in landmass, in 1865 Canada's population was about 10% of the United States and about to become smaller. Canada was elevated to the status of being a British dominion in 1867, making it a virtually independent polity. Some 25% of Canadians didn't see this as creating a positive environment and emigrated to the United States. Many were French Catholics fearing rule by "unsupervised" Protestant British-Canadians.

In 1885 Canada implemented a head tax on Chinese immigrants that severely curtailed Chinese immigration. This policy was the first of many over the next seventy years that restricted immigrants by their country of origin. Canada too wanted to limit diversity. They wanted to maintain a majority that was white, Christian (Protestant), with origins in northern Europe.

---

[112] Whites included other non-blacks. Among the white category, Mexicans were nearly half.

[113] Lynchings were most common in the southern United States, and blacks were the most common victims. Whites were more commonly victims in the western United States.

[114] In hindsight, the Chinese Exclusion Act, like other immigration laws, has been cast as a racist policy. But all immigration policies can be framed as racist. Nations that virtually exclude immigrants could be framed as the most racist. Immigration policies are the prerogative of sovereign nations. They have the right to control their borders and decide who can become citizens. Without this, it would be impossible to govern for too many reasons to cite here.

The American Industrial Revolution created additional needs for labor that was easily met by the millions from the south and center of Europe seeking safety and work. In the Russian Empire, there were Jewish pogroms and the Russian Civil War (1917–1922). Several European countries were experiencing hyperinflation, and WWI was inflicting mass carnage across Europe and the Ottoman and Russian empires. In total nearly 25 million immigrants arrived in the United States mostly from Italy, Greece, Hungary, Poland, and Russia including 1.75 million Jews escaping persecution in the Russian Empire (mainly from Poland and Ukraine).[clxxxviii]

This massive influx of non-northern European immigrants created unsettling levels of diversity that affected both Americans and the immigrants. The Ku Klux Klan (KKK) resurged in 1915 as the prototypical white supremacist organization, even though it also targeted many whites. The resurgence was motivated by the tens of millions of Irish Catholics, Italian Catholics, other mostly south and central European Orthodox Catholics, and Jews that had been immigrating to the United States, in addition to blacks organizing for civil rights.[115] While few in number, Jews had escaped discrimination; now that changed. The Klan despised Jews, Catholics, and blacks. They despised half the US population. This incarnation of the Klan lasted ten years. The KKK's benevolent programs couldn't outweigh member intolerance for violence.

It wasn't just the Klan targeting the Jews. Others, like Henry Ford, founder of the Ford Motor Company, used his newspaper, the Dearborn Independent, to run 91 issues to blame the Jews for America's ills. "The rhetoric was not unusual for its content, as much as its scope."[clxxxix] Ford was successful in driving growth of antisemitism movements in the United States.

The Immigration Act of 1924 was not a response to the Klan, but rather a response to the concerns of many Americans. The Act banned immigrants from Asia and nearly everywhere else but northern Europe. The deluge of immigrants from central and southern Europe was brought to a virtual standstill. Meanwhile discrimination against non-northern Europeans already living in the United States remained high. Discrimination against Italians was particularly virulent, and not just to those in an indentured state. Pseudo-scientific theories emerged of Mediterranean people being inferior humans.

While many Italian-Americans (and Japanese-Americans) bravely fought in the US military during WWII, 600,000 undocumented Italians were "detained, relocated, stripped of their property or placed under curfew."[cxc] About 3,000 were placed in internment camps. For the Japanese, 120,000 were interned and 80,000 were citizens. About 11,000 Germans were also interned. The choice of these ethnic groups was not random. Italy, Japan and Germany were the three primary Axis Powers in WWII.[116] The greater population of interned Japanese was not random either. Pearl Harbor left an indelible mark. Ninety percent of Japanese-Canadians were also interned during WWII. In 1988, both the United States and Canada provided compensation to Japanese *survivors* of the detention camps.

---

[115] In 1909 the NAACP (National Association for the Advancement of Colored People) was organized.
[116] During the war it was common practice among all belligerents to intern immigrants and descendants from enemy countries. There was a fear they could be conduits for information helpful to the enemies.

Between independence and 1945 the landmass of the United States had grown nearly tenfold, and the population 56-fold. The population was a composite of diverse ethnicities, but it had become increasingly homogenous. About 10 percent were black. Nearly 90% were white and Christian, and mostly English speaking and culturally American. The latter two were missing for some European ethnicities because they had not yet assimilated.

**The brutal bargain of integration.** The Americanization process is gradual, and it is not forced. It relies on immigrants wanting to integrate or assimilate. For the Italians and Irish this took multiple generations and it was filled with angst, and feelings of displacement from abandoning ethnic traditions. Ironically, assimilating or integrating into America does not call for abandoning ethnic traditions and celebrations.[cxci] Still, perceptions can overtake reality.

Integrating is a hard choice, but it offers the chance to forever exit the discomfort of ghettoes or slums marred by poverty and violence. Key to every ethnic group integrating and ending discrimination was endeavoring to modify their ethnic stereotypes. In the early 20th century, the Irish, Italians, and blacks were all competing for the same low-status jobs.[cxcii] They also had the same stereotype: dangerous, ignorant, lazy, law breakers. These characteristics were in conflict with the American Creed. The Creed defined an American identity in 1945 as English speaking, [117] a hard work ethic, individualism (self-reliant),[118] belief in the rule of law, Christian, and the duty to create heaven on earth. [lxvii,119]

When it came to identifying as American, all three groups were Christian, but the Irish and Italians were Catholic. Christian really meant Protestant. More Irish and blacks spoke English, but accents and dialects were more likely to be ridiculed than valued. The Irish had to get past seven centuries of racism in Britain. For the Italians and blacks, racism was more recent. Being white wasn't an advantage for the Irish because they weren't considered white. Into the late 19th century, the Irish were being dehumanized and depicted as apes, living in Irish community squalor.[cxciii] The Italians were similarly depicted as non-white, and also violent, murderous gangsters.

Throughout its history America has been viewed as a land of opportunity by people all over the world. Most and the best opportunities have been available to people who identified and were identified as Americans. The process of assimilating or integrating has been called a brutal bargain. How do you get from being seen as dangerous, ignorant, lazy, law breakers to being seen as law abiding, self-reliant, hard-working, English speakers? Accepting the so-called brutal bargain. Many American immigrants came from nations where repression was stifling, with no possibility to exit poverty, and scant opportunities to realize dreams. Many were motivated to jump at the unique chance to engage in any type of bargain that would

---

[117] In the mid-19th century, the Gaelic language was being subordinated to English as the primary language in Ireland. Irish people that spoke English often had a strong accent (brogue) that was difficult for Americans to understand.

[118] Individualism is a belief in being self-reliant. This is in contrast to a reliance on the state.

[119] The United States government endeavored to assimilate Native Americans into the American Creed. It was viewed by the government as the best means to resolve the challenge of managing populations struggling with a unique autonomous status in combination with government oversight and assistance. Some Native American tribes were supportive, but others were not. The latter could not see value in assimilating. They clung to a biased image of whites as land stealers.

end a brutal existence for them and their descendants. Honoring the bargain is central to ending conscious and unconscious discrimination that impedes access to opportunities. Every different population in America has faced discrimination until they have adopted an American identity.

## US & Canada - Racism and anti-Racism after 1945

No person invested more in ending the formal or informal subordination of select populations in the world than US President Franklin Delano Roosevelt (1933-1945). He parlayed American military victory in WWII to end the subordination of populations to imperial powers and to gain national commitments to end discrimination. He triggered a new zeitgeist on subordination; it was immoral. His successor, President Harry Truman (1945-1953), demonstrated his alignment. America became the first woke nation and it has maintained its position of anti-racist leadership ever since.

The list of significant programs, policies and laws in the United States that specifically address discrimination is very long. The commitments from Americas national leaders, and corporate chieftains is even more impressive. Affirmative action programs first implemented under FDR have been renewed from one presidential administration to the next. Truman established the President's Committee on Civil Rights, which later resulted in a permanent Commission on Civil Rights. In the 1940s the courts were becoming very active in declaring laws that called for segregation unconstitutional. In 1948 Truman made it illegal to discriminate in civilian agencies and ordered desegregation in the military. President Dwight Eisenhower (1953-1961) appointed Earl Warren as the Chief Justice of the US Supreme Court paving the way for landmark civil rights legislation, including Brown v the Board of Education (1952) that made it clear separate (segregation) was never equal. The 1960s was a very busy time for new laws, executive orders, congressional acts, and court rulings solidifying America's commitment to anti-discrimination, and eliminating ambiguity on the illegality of discrimination in employment, pay, housing, and lending; and denying anyone (but prisoners) the right to vote.

In 1963, President John F. Kennedy (JFK) addressed the nation. "Race has no place in American life or law." "It's time for America to fulfill its promise that all men are created equal." He called on Congress to pass comprehensive civil rights legislation and he called on all Americans to address inequality. "But legislation, I repeat, cannot solve this problem alone. It must be solved in the homes of every American in every community across our country."

It is no coincidence that a man that became symbolic of the end of three centuries of anti-Irishism and anti-Catholicism to become the first Catholic and Irish president understood the enormous challenges to ending racism in any form. During his campaign "anti-Mickism" and anti-Catholicism was everywhere and included "hooded 'patriots' burning crosses in the night." It was just three years earlier in 1960 that JFK was appealing to the nation to end religious intolerance that had plagued the nation since the 17<sup>th</sup> century.[cxciv]

"I believe in an America where religious intolerance will someday end; where all men and all churches are treated as equal; where every man has the same right to attend or not attend the church of his choice; where there is no Catholic vote, no anti-Catholic vote, no bloc voting of any kind; and where Catholics, Protestants and Jews will refrain from those attitudes of disdain and division…and promote instead the American ideal of brotherhood." John F. Kennedy, September 12, 1960.

JFK knew that governments could pass laws, make commitments to all men being created equal, and offer protections for freedom of religion, but they could not end religious or racial intolerance. Governments cannot control what people think. For this he saw a greater role with parents – not some parents, all parents.

It is also no coincidence that anti-racist champion JFK encouraged Saudi Arabia to end the Arab slave trade in 1962, and was aligned with America's civil rights movement led by Dr. Martin Luther King. In 1963, tens of thousands of Americans, both black and white were mesmerized by King's speech at the Lincoln Memorial.

"In the process of gaining our rightful place, we must not be guilty of wrongful deeds. Let us not seek to satisfy our thirst for freedom by drinking from the cup of bitterness and hatred. We must forever conduct our struggle on the high plane of dignity and discipline. We must not allow our creative protest to degenerate into physical violence… The marvelous new militancy which has engulfed the Negro community must not lead us to a distrust of all white people, for many of our white brothers, as evidenced by their presence here today, have come to realize that their destiny is tied up with our destiny. And they have come to realize that their freedom is inextricably bound to our freedom…We can never be satisfied as long as the Negro is the victim of the unspeakable horrors of police brutality. We can never be satisfied as long as our bodies, heavy with the fatigue of travel, cannot gain lodging in the motels of the highways and the hotels of the cities. We cannot be satisfied as long as the negro's basic mobility is from a smaller ghetto to a larger one. We can never be satisfied as long as our children are stripped of their self-hood and robbed of their dignity by signs stating: "For Whites Only." We cannot be satisfied as long as a Negro in Mississippi cannot vote and a Negro in New York believes he has nothing for which to vote…

I have a dream that one day this nation will rise up and live out the true meaning of its creed: "We hold these truths to be self-evident, that all men are created equal."
*Dr. Martin Luther King. I Have a Dream. August 28, 1963.*

King raised awareness throughout the country to racial inequality and was given the Noble Peace Prize in 1964 for using nonviolent resistance.

Kennedy was assassinated in 1963, five years before King was assassinated. JFK's successor, President Lyndon Johnson, with his close southern connections, ensured passage of the 1964 Civil Rights Act. This Act outlawed employment discrimination based on race, color, sex, religion or national origin, prohibited racial segregation at work, and school, and ensured equal application of voter registration requirements. Passage of the Act also motivated a brief and unsuccessful resurgence of the KKK.[cxcv]

In 1964 and 1965 the Great Society and War on Poverty were launched. The goals were abolishing inequality, ending poverty, and reducing crime. This initiated massive government assistance programs that today allocates nearly $1 trillion annually to help disadvantaged groups.

Instead of a focus on assimilating Native Americans, which was partially successful,[120] legislation was passed in the 1960s and 1970s to provide additional government funded services to facilitate education and health care on Native American reservations.[121] The nation was switching its focus to a multicultural policy for Native Americans that did not want to integrate. Canada similarly changed its direction in the 80s and 90s away from assimilating Native Canadians and toward facilitating autonomy.[122]

Autonomous or not, neither Canada nor the United States washed their hands of old or new issues related to their indigenous populations. In the United States historical land transactions with the Native Americans were believed to be agreed upon, however an issue of unfair power relationships left lingering feelings in some of land theft. To address this, the United States set up between 1946 and 1978 the Indian Claims Commission. After this, claims continued to be negotiated with lawsuits. By 2016 about $7 billion in claims had been paid. Some point out that Native Americans have gained much more financially from the special concession granted to run casinos. More than $30 billion in gaming revenue was generated in 2017 alone. In 1973, Canada similarly set up a commission to compensate claims of non-payment of land for Native Canadians. As to gaming, Native Canadians wish they had the same rights as Native Americans. And most indigenous people wish they had been treated like Native Americans and Native Canadians.

In most countries, the rights and land of indigenous populations have been disregarded. To try to remedy this, in 2006 the United Nations passed the United Declarations on the Rights of Indigenous People. This declaration is an attempt to protect the land and other freedoms to over three hundred million indigenous people that have been denied their land and been uprooted in parts of Asia, Africa and South America. Unfortunately, UN declarations lack the force of law and indigenous people continue to be displaced without warning, compensation, or resettlement.

It was also in the 1960s that immigration laws were overhauled. The United States would no longer give preferences based on national origin. While many new nations created zero immigration policies and were encouraging foreign populations

---

[120] About 22% of Native Americans live on reservations.

[121] Autonomy has not been a solution for the challenges Native Americans face. The 22% of Native Americans that live on reservations experience greater hardships than most that have chosen to enter mainstream America. Those that have assimilated into more populous areas also express fewer perceptions of discrimination.

[122] Both Native American and Native Canadian children were transported, often large distances to attend public schools. Although, this practice did result in many assimilating, it was lambasted as cruel. Today reservations in both countries have autonomy over education that is financially supported by the American and Canadian governments.

to leave, not uncommonly with expulsion orders and highly discriminatory practices, the United States was a leader in opening its doors to immigrants from all over the world. Canada did similarly. This new zeitgeist to non-discriminatory immigration policies assumed the more or less natural process of integration would continue to be the eventual solution to discrimination against new immigrants. America's "melting pot," which encouraged diverse populations to peacefully and productively coexist as fellow nationals was unique and admired around the globe.

In the 1960s, fifty years after Catholics had become the nation's largest religious denomination, discrimination was fast-fading against America's Irish Catholics, in addition to Italian-Americans (also Catholic), and German-Americans (many Catholic).[123] Historian Arthur Schlesinger (1888-1965) called the discrimination against Catholics "the deepest bias in the history of the American people." Bias against Catholics also had a long history in Canada. Catholics faced legal discrimination until Catholic Emancipation in 1829 but it persisted in less fervent forms into the mid 20th century.

Many Americans might point to African-Americans or Native-Americans, rather than Catholics, as having deeper biases. But these biases today are unacceptable. Deep biases against Catholics remain acceptable and covert.[cxcvi] The same can be said for women. Do the biases for any of these groups look the same as in 1945? Not even close.

Outside Catholic biases, the biases against Irish-, Italian- and German Americans is imperceptible. Fading discrimination for these ethnic groups appears to have a tie to the 1960s Civil Rights movement. New programs to facilitate a level playing field were focusing on race, and not the white race. These hyphenated groups were competing for jobs with blacks, who they now saw as having preferences. They were motivated to integrate to end discrimination that kept them in the ghettoes and slums and away from better opportunities. They succeeded.[cxcvii]

Employment-related diversity programs first took off in the 1960s. Consistent with increasing diversity from immigration and more women in the workforce, these programs were supercharged in the 1980s and 1990s. These efforts have been paying dividends in minority and female employment, promotions, training, income, and occupations.[124] Educational institutions also instituted affirmative action-type admissions policies to ensure student body diversity. When they were challenged as discriminatory, the courts ruled that universities were within their rights to consider diversity as a criterion. [cxcviii] America's institutions were clearly demonstrating their commitments to anti-discrimination.

Still in 1990, Louis Farrakhan, the leader of the separatist Nation of Islam, saw progress for blacks going backward. Was it going backward due to discrimination? This was not evident. Performance at school was going backward, and this could lead to negative progress, but this was not tied to discrimination.[cxcix] It was more likely to be tied to the stalling of racial integration and a dramatic increase in black single parent households. In 1950 this was 22% but in 1990 it was 52%.[cc] Farrakhan

---

[123] Discrimination against the Germans had resurged as a result of WWI and WWII.

[124] Critics of affirmative action and diversity programs argue that they are discriminatory toward white men and women. Advocates cite the need to facilitate integration that can change and ultimately end unconscious biases. The advocates are winning.

promoted another Back to Africa movement. He wanted the government to purchase lands in Africa as a form of restitution so African-Americans could start their own nation, really a second nation. Liberia was first. He saw this as a mutually beneficial solution for Africa and African-Americans. The most educated black population in the world could help Africa. "Africans helped sell us into slavery. And so Africa should bear some responsibility in helping us to get out of the condition that we are in." [cci] Did he believe that Africa would be remorseful and want to remedy their pivotal role in the slave trade? Did he know that slavery was still condoned in many parts of Africa? Did he believe that developing-African nations had the financial wherewithal to allocate monies to programs to support African-Americans that in 1990 had 10 times the buying power of Nigerians (26 times the amount of real income). Did he know that 59% of the global poor live in Black Africa? Did he believe that Africa would be discrimination free because everyone was black? Did he believe Africa would be a better place for blacks to prosper than America?

One can only imagine that Farrakhan was like so many other Americans. Unaware of the complexities involved in creating a multiracial nation with equal opportunities for all. Unaware that it's never been done. Unaware that only a small percentage of nations are even trying. Unaware that African-Americans are the most educated and prosperous black population in the world. Unaware that most nations find discrimination useful. Unaware that Africans were queuing up to immigrate to America in search of better opportunities. Unaware that the United States was then and remains the leading anti-racist nation.

## Racism and anti-Racism - 21st Century America

America's leading anti-racist position became global news in 2008. The world's largest economy and most populous white-majority nation elected a black man to the highest position in the land.[125] Many believed that Americans would not elect a black man president. Apparently, most Americans didn't see a black man. Analyzing America's voting patterns, researchers concluded that "the race of the candidate didn't seem to play a role one way or the other."[ccii]

The outcome was even more amazing because Obama's spiritual adviser, the Reverend Jeremiah Wight, was anti-Jewish, openly preached God damn America, and accused the US of creating HIV to eradicate blacks. He was a racist. On March 18, 2008 Obama did distance himself from some of Wright's positions. "The remarks that have caused this recent firestorm weren't simply controversial. They weren't simply a religious leader's effort to speak out against perceived injustice. Instead, they expressed a profoundly distorted view of this country - a view that sees white racism as endemic."

Having a black man as president was helpful to addressing discrimination against blacks because Obama could communicate with blacks in a way that a white leader could not. Obama thought many problems blacks face were unrelated to race,

---

[125] Next closest was Peru, ranked 48th economically and 43rd by population. Peruvians elected Japanese-Peruvian Alberto Fujimori.

unrelated to discrimination, and solvable by blacks. He called on blacks to do their part.

> We know that more than half of all black children live in single-parent households [it was 65% in 2018], a number that has doubled — doubled — since we were children.[126] We know the statistics — that children who grow up without a father are five times more likely to live in poverty and commit crime; nine times more likely to drop out of schools and twenty times more likely to end up in prison. They are more likely to have behavioral problems, or run away from home or become teenage parents themselves. And the foundations of our community are weaker because of it.
>
> Yes, we need more money for our schools, and more outstanding teachers in the classroom, and more after-school programs for our children. Yes, we need more jobs and more job training and more opportunity in our communities. But we also need families to raise our children.
>
> Barack Obama, June 15, 2008.

Obama could have struck an even sharper note by elaborating on behavioral problems. Children growing up without a father are 4.7 times more likely to suffer mood disorders, they are also more likely to do drugs, be involved with gangs, be depressed, have feelings of worthlessness, be obese,[127] be victims of child abuse, and be prone toward anger and hostility. [cciii,cciv,128]

Many non-black Americans saw the election of Obama as proof positive that the final chapter on racism had been written. Many around the world agreed. Only a non-racist white nation would elect a black man to be president and only a non-racist nation would have an army of globally prominent African-Americans in all facets of life: Hollywood, business, medicine, academia, government, and sports.

Some argued that having the most educated and prosperous black community in the world was a distraction from the issue that all black people did not have equal opportunities because they faced discrimination. This was plainly evident in black household income being about 40% lower than for whites. Was it plainly evident? Some pointed to blacks having far more single parent households. Different studies show this negatively affects household income by 11-62%, with an average of 32%. Single parent households are nearly 3 times more common in black families as whites. [ccv] Some also noted that half of the black population lived in the states with the lowest pay scales – the south. Per capita incomes in most southern states are about 40% less than the average for the country. Combine per capita income differences by location with a high percentage of single parent households and a significant portion of the differences in household income are explained. Still, this

---

[126] Single parent households for Native Americans was 53%, Latinos 40%, whites 24%, and blacks 65%. This data is from the Annie E Casey Foundation.

[127] Childhood obesity is 50% higher in single parent v two parent households. Obesity counts among the most powerful instigators of discrimination.

[128] These problems do not apply only to blacks; they are applicable to people who grow up without fathers. See footnote above for relevant percentages by race.

data didn't alter the position that racism was the reason blacks had fewer opportunities.

There were, however, other arguments against racism as the instigator of unequal opportunities. These included the influence of educational attainment, skill levels, self-segregation, proximity to high paying jobs, declining quality of public educations, and increased competition from other minorities and women. There were also debates about aspects of public assistance that might be exacerbating discrimination by accentuating subordination. Benevolently racist programs and practices "presumably help, empower, or protect communities of color [but] can often support and reinforce…inadvertently—a system of racial domination." [ccvi]

Many programs supporting the War on Poverty meet the test of being benevolently racist and cementing recipients into a subordinated role in society where opportunities are fewer. Since launching War on Poverty programs in the 1960s marriage rates for blacks, Latinos, and Native Americans has plummeted and out-of-wedlock births and single-parent families have soared. Also soaring is the number of people receiving and the amount spent on public assistance. In 2012, 13.2% of non-Hispanic white Americans, 42% of blacks, and 36% of Latinos received public assistance.[ccvii] Kay C. James, president of the Heritage Foundation, noted that it's become common for fathers to reject parental responsibilities. "Nearly 1 million black boys and girls are being raised by a grandparent." "The welfare state … substitute[d] a check for a father, a social worker for a caring mother or grandmother, and a slew of civil rights organizations for the neighborhood church." [ccviii] Trillions of dollars in public assistance have been spent on programs to level the playing field. They have helped to raise many from poverty, but by encouraging people to be single parents, to live in segregated communities, not to seek better opportunities outside their communities, and not to further their educations, they have also inadvertently reinforced racial dominance.

Is it possible that the perception that blacks didn't have equality of opportunity was driven by increasing competition? When the Civil Rights Act of 1964 was enacted, blacks were 10.5% of the population, Latinos were 3%, Asians 0.5%, and mixed race 0%. When it came to increasing diversity, private and public organizations focused on blacks. Over time, blacks became one of many focal points. America's newer immigration policy dramatically diversified the nation. A nation that was 87% white in 1964, in 2020 was 60% non-Hispanic white, 17% Latino, 13.4% black, 5.9% Asian, 1.2% Native American, and 2.5% mixed race.[129,130] When it came to the workforce, there was another huge change. The participation rate of women had doubled between 1964 and 2019. It had gone from 38.3% to 76.8%. Women also faced discrimination in the workplace, and they were competing for opportunities and diversity targets in the public and private sectors.

**Self-segregation and integration.** What about the impact of self-segregation on equality of opportunity? America's legal system from the 1940s to 1960s made sure that segregation was illegal. It had become clear that there was no separate but equal.

---

[129] Mixed race in 1960 wasn't counted. Today, mixed race populations are understated because the United States is unusual in counting and seeing mulattoes as black, and because many mixed-raced Latinos identify as white. This is a common practice in Latam.

[130] Canada's newer immigration policy has led to significant changes in diversity too. It was now 83% white, 9% Asian, 3.5% black and 4.5% Native Canadians.

But the government cannot prevent minorities from self-segregating. If people prefer to live and socialize among like people, even if it diminishes opportunities, that is their right. Self-segregation is self-selected multiculturalism that places a priority on preserving differences and inadvertently decrements the priority on economic outcomes. One data point on self-segregated outcomes is cities with the highest segregation of blacks and whites have the greatest rates of black poverty. Latinos that self-segregate also experience diminished economic outcomes.[ccix,131] Multiculturalism and self-segregation are anti-formulas for building equitable multiracial states.

Segregated black communities are most common in the south, where, per the 2010 Census, 54% of blacks live. If that seems high, it was 90% in 1900. Millions of black people in multiple migrations between 1910 and 1970 moved to other parts of the country that offered more and better opportunities. A sharp slowdown in migrating occurred coincident with War on Poverty programs. They may have lessened the motivation for people to move for better opportunities. Cities in the west and Midwest have found the best integration outcomes for blacks and whites, and the best economic opportunities for blacks. In all of these states the black population is less than 7%. [ccx,ccxi,ccxii] The best economic mobility for blacks is in the north and west, but blacks tend to live in regions where "upward mobility is relatively low.[ccxiii] Self-segregation was not working for Native Americans either. According to the US Census, depending on the reservation, poverty can be twice as high as for Native Americans overall.[132]

For all ethnic groups, integration is key to lessening discrimination and expanding access to opportunities. Georgetown University law professor, Sheryll Cashin, has written on the failures of blacks and whites to integrate. She notes that 85% of whites are indifferent to the skin color of their neighbors. (In 2013, the World Values Survey placed it at over 95%.[ccxiv] ) What they care about is the quality of schools their children attend, crime rates, public services, and stable property values. These are the same things that middle-class black people care about. This has led both groups to live as neighbors. Blacks and whites with similar goals, values, and income levels tend to integrate well.

Cashin notes that "even at the height of the civil rights era, socializing with whites was never a goal in itself for black people, and undoubtedly for many, it is not one today." [ccxv] Perhaps, but it seems like Martin Luther King thought it should be. "People fail to get along because they fear each other; they fear each other because they don't know each other; they don't know each other because they have not communicated with each other." Integration is the antidote to this fear.

Socializing with whites might not be a goal for many blacks, but this doesn't mean blacks reject the benefits of integration. A study by Pew Research found that African-Americans more than any other group, by a margin of 19 points, thought it was more important to go to a racially and ethnically mixed school than a more homogenous school in their community. Blacks were also most likely to say they

---

[131] Segregated Cuban communities did not have higher poverty.
[132] On 8 out of 10 of the largest reservations, the percentage living in poverty was 41-59%. Rates of poverty in predominantly black or Latino communities can be similarly high.

wanted more racial diversity in their communities. [ccxvi] Cashin noted that the desired diversity was in *their* neighborhoods. Still, slowly but surely blacks, whites, Asians, and Latinos are successfully integrating. [ccxvii,ccxviii,ccxix] More than 95% of Americans don't care what race their neighbors are. The days when some whites would move when non-whites moved into their neighborhood has been relegated to history. America today is unrecognizable from the days of the Black Codes and Jim Crow laws.

The pace of integration has stagnated, but this is less a function of discrimination and more a preference to live with like people. There is considerable research that shows the positive effects on income, education, and crime when moving to neighborhoods with low poverty, which commonly means more whites and Asians. But many don't care to live in these neighborhoods. The US government has invested in many programs to encourage low-income African-Americans and Latinos to move to integrated neighborhoods that offer superior opportunities. What they have found is that people instead move to like neighborhoods, and in some cases use vouchers to return to their old neighborhoods. When people have chosen this path, positive improvements in education for their children, or family income did not materialize. [ccxx,ccxxi]

Self-segregation for blacks, Latinos or Native Americans, may reduce perceptions of discrimination in their communities that can make life more comfortable, but it does not create safer communities, better schools, improve educational outcomes, or create a foundation for better economic opportunities. To the contrary, crime is higher, quality of education is lower and dropout rates are higher in high school and college. [ccxxii,ccxxiii,ccxxiv] Many cite the challenges for poorer people to move, although the continuous arrival of millions of poorer immigrants to America indicates that desires for better opportunities can lead to accepting and surmounting challenges. Still, government programs have shown that given the means low-income blacks and Latinos were inclined to choose the comfort of segregated communities over the chance for better schools and economic opportunities.

Leaving the comfort of living with like people is part of the brutal bargain. But if the goal is equality of opportunity, forced or self-imposed segregation does not work, and there is a long list of supportive data points from all over the world. Granted, integrating is hard. In the 20th century half of Italian immigrants returned to Italy rather than change. For those Italians that accepted the bargain, their ancestors can only express appreciation. This becomes especially evident when a visit to the home country yields the realization that Italy is a land where people that are successful have connections. That's true in a lot of countries. In these countries, parents don't tell their children if they work hard, they can be whomever they want to be.

War on Poverty programs were unhelpful to encouraging integration and so are the conclusions drawn by Ibram X. Kendi, a scholar on race at Boston University, and 2019 best-selling author of How to be an Antiracist. He said that integrating with whites robs black people of their identity. He accused whites of "lynching black culture." Does the identity of an American as English speaking, self-reliant, embracing a hard work ethic, and accepting the inherent equality of rule of law, lynch blacks or anyone of their culture?

If not integration with whites, then what? Self-segregation, self-imposed multiculturalism? Every implementation of multiculturalism from South African apartheid, to Europe's isolation of migrant workers, and the use of "reservations" or "nations" for New World indigenous populations has failed. In multiracial societies, there is no separate but equal.

Integration stands alone as the one proven way multiracial nations can successfully build national identities that end discrimination and deliver equality of opportunity. Irish-Americans and Italian-Americans are a testament to the power of integration. More recently Asian-Americans, Latino-Americans, and Asian-Canadians have been undergoing or progressing integration with good outcomes. [ccxxv,] [133] This has been taking place even with levels of discrimination for Asians and Latinos that was similar to blacks.[ccxxvi] Good outcomes are reflected in the steady flow of Asian and Latino immigrants to America. In 2018, Latino-born immigrants numbered 20 million, and Asian immigrants 12 million.[134,ccxxvii] Asian-Americans and Asian-Canadians have fared extra well. They are the minority groups that are most socially integrated, and they are the most highly compensated racial groups in America and Canada. Most successful of all are the Indian-Americans. While Asian-Americans have household incomes 25% higher than whites, for Indian-Americans it is 60%. Latinos though have not done too badly, and integration has helped. In 2020 the GDP of US Latinos was higher than any country in Latin America. There are 59 million US Latinos. The population of Brazil is 210 million. [ccxxviii]

There is also data for improved outcomes for blacks that integrate, for example superior economic outcomes in the west where blacks and whites have integrated well. Superior economic outcomes for blacks in states where black populations are less concentrated.[ccxxix] Another possible data point on improved outcomes comes from black immigrants (vs. US origin blacks). There is insufficient data that is specific to how the integration of black immigrants affects economic outcomes. But it is known that black immigrants are much more likely to live in the west or the north where economic mobility is higher and concentrated black communities are fewer, and data supports better outcomes. Relative to US origin blacks, black immigrants have household incomes that are on average 31% higher. They are 37% more likely to have a college degree, and 39% more likely to be married. They are also less likely to hold deep seated biases against whites. The number of black immigrants to America has been skyrocketing from black majority nations in sub-Saharan Africa, and the Caribbean. In 2018 there were 4.8 million foreign-born blacks in the United States.[ccxxx,135] It can easily be that America to these black immigrants is a land where blacks can dream big, like being president, CEO, or the richest woman in the world. Dreams they couldn't have at home.[ccxxxi] They see America as a land of opportunity.

---

[133] Most Asian-Americans and Asian-Canadians strongly identify with the United States and Canada respectively. They also identify with the cultures of their descendants. This is also true of many Latinos. To some degree it is true of multigenerational hyphenated white Americans and Canadians, but it has diminished over time. This is an outcome of assimilation. Dr. Peter Skerry of Boston College presents assimilation as having economic, social, cultural and political components. Most often the component immigrants hold onto is cultural.

[134] Beginning in 2015 Asian immigrants began to outnumber Latinos.

[135] Immigrants from sub-Saharan Africa have increased 300% since 2000, and 1500% since 1980. There has been a similar increase for blacks from the Caribbean.

# Re-diagnosing the challenges

The rapid increases in diversity in America has been extraordinary, and so has the progress people of color and women have been making to close gaps in equality. Progress has not been a deterrent to American politicians, social organizers, academics, and other leaders re-diagnosing the challenges of discrimination, particularly against blacks. There is an army of data to support their re-assessments. Chief among the cited data sources is the Implicit Association Test (IAT). Tests have been taken over twenty million times. About 75% of test takers for the skin-color test score "biases" against people with darker skin.[ccxxxii] (The same percentage was found for "biases" against women.) Dozens of writers for popular presses have concluded that racism (and sexism) is everywhere.[ccxxxiii] America wasn't making progress; it was a hell hole of racism.

It turns out that the IAT skin-color test does not measure discrimination; it measures preferences. The preference someone has for the company of people that have light skin or dark skin. It turns out more people, on a slightly declining basis are more comfortable with light skinned people. But then again at least 75% of the people that have taken the test are light skinned. About 50% of blacks were also found to have a preference for light skinned people. [ccxxxiv,ccxxxv,ccxxxvi,ccxxxvii] In the United States the preference for light skinned people was not very strong compared to other nations. It ranked 94th out of 146 countries. Its preference was the weakest of all light-skinned majority countries in the world except Andorra and Albania. [ccxxxviii]

People preferring to be with someone that is light- or dark-skinned is hardly a measure of racism. Studies abound that show people like to be with like people, and very importantly this does not correlate with racial hostility or racism.[ccxxxix] Do these preferences result in discriminatory acts? Rarely. Even the researchers that developed the IAT admit there is a very weak correlation between the unconscious preferences measured by the IAT score and discriminatory behaviors. [ccxl, ccxli]

The Black Live Matter movement (BLM) that began in 2012 and was supercharged in 2020 coincided with the new theme for why people believe blacks do not have equality of opportunity. America is a systemically and structurally racist country and blacks are its victims. Not all people of color – just blacks. The theme has become an uncontestable narrative. Anyone disagreeing is a racist. Anyone advocating for the integration of blacks is a racist.[ccxlii] Anyone pointing to the prominence of blacks in all walks of life is a racist. People who disagreed with some of BLMs official or unofficial positions, like de-emphasizing the nuclear family, or leanings toward Marxism is a racist. Anyone objecting to equating police and their supporters to white supremacists is a racist.[136] Supporters of Israel are racists. Drawing attention to the relationship between policing and crime is racist. Saying all lives mattered is racist. [ccxliii,ccxliv] Drawing analogies between the discrimination faced by Italian- and Irish-Americans is racist. Ironically, the results of a survey published in 2020 found the analogy quite relevant. The survey question was: "Irish, Italians, Jewish and many other minorities overcame prejudice and worked their way up.

---

[36] According to Pew Research, Americans (82%) overwhelmingly support police and think they treat all people equally. This percentage includes a black population where 48% believe police are racists.

Blacks should do the same without any special favors." Only one-third of the blacks surveyed disagreed. [ccxlv]

In the midst of the 2020 BLM protests there was more data to support the narrative. A poll was conducted to see if people thought racial and ethnic discrimination was a big problem in America. Seventy-six percent said they thought it was, up from 51% in 2015.[ccxlvi] The mainstream media seized on the poll to say racism was an increasing problem. That's not what the poll indicated. When people are fed a steady uncontested diet of racism, racism, racism, and the nation's cities are experiencing nightly BLM protests it would be hard for people not to perceive racism as a big problem. But the survey does not say that 76% of Americans are racist, that America is systemically racist, or that racism in America is increasing. It could not say that, because the data does not support that.

There was more support for the narrative from University of Washington professor, Robin D'Angelo. During the 2020 BLM protests, her book White Fragility, was flying off the shelves. She wrote. "all white people are invested in and collude with racism." A white person that disagrees is a fragile white person – racist implied. This harmful message resonated. All whites are racists, period, end of story, no discussion.

Turn on the news, read a paper, there is a steady drumbeat of systemic racist America. To keep the narrative intact, self-censorship of opposing views seems evident. There seems to be this alignment with critical race theory that jettisons objectivity to deliver their version of moral clarity. Instead of reporting news, there has been clarification of *their* view on the morality or immorality of news. Was it morality or politics? Understating progress and tying it to discrimination, and painting whites as born racists has been noted as a political ploy to aggrandize power.[ccxlvii, ccxlviii] Academics seemed to be supporting political goals, or was it book sales? It's hard to know, which academic has been making the job of addressing racism harder. Is it Kendi or D'Angelo? When ideas resonate, like whites are lynching black culture, casting white people that adopt black orphans as racist baby stealers, or saying all white people collude with racism, how does that advance anti-racism? It doesn't.

When embellishing on discrimination became useful to politicians and academics, and the media became a bedfellow, addressing it really became complicated.

## Censoring opposing views

The new diagnosis of what ails blacks as racism, racism, racism has become an uncontested narrative for the mainstream media. The Economist was unique as a liberal "mainstream" magazine in emphasizing a problem that has been growing in America for years. Silencing critics. It is a powerful vehicle to discriminate against diversity of thought. Silencing critics is the tool of dictatorships not liberal democracies. But this has been occurring in America. In this case, white opponents with superior credentials had no chance to weigh in on the narrative because they didn't know what it was like to be black. But black leaders with opposing views like Jason Riley and Dr. Michael Javen Fortner from the Manhattan Institute, Dr. Glenn Loury from Brown University, Columbia professor, Dr. John McWhorter, all-American Herschel Walker, and Ayaan Hirsi Ali from Stanford were being silenced by the mainstream media. These people were branded as sell outs, traitors or Uncle Toms, or per Spike Lee, "they aren't regular black people." The muffled voice of Ali said, "America is the best place on the planet to be a black… I have never come across a society so determined to end racism. If you want to argue this, travel and see for yourself."[ccxlix,137]

It was a local paper in Missouri that published this comment about the horrible death of George Floyd. It was from Larry Elder, a black conservative leader. "Minneapolis in 2020 is not Birmingham, Alabama, in the '50s. The top cop is not a racist segregationist like Birmingham's infamous Bull Connor, who sicced dogs and turned water hoses on civil rights protesters. The police chief of Minneapolis is Mexican-American and black. The mayor is a young Democratic liberal. The district's U.S. House representative is black. The vice president of the city council is black, as is the state attorney general."[ccl]

No media outlet bothered to pick up a 2020 study indicating that America in 2000 is not America in 2020. An often-quoted study today is from 2003. It found that the name Jamal on a resume rather than John led to fewer interviews.[ccli] In a 2020 study, Malik Washington was favored for an interview over Christopher Wu, William Schmitt, and Jose Vasquez. Just as relevant there were no names that generated a strong bias.[cclii]

Dr. Michael Javen Fortner, and the author of the Black Silent Majority wrote on July 5, 2020: "Analysis of racism has been transformed from a set of observations and falsifiable propositions into its own epistemology: a way of knowing that bends reality to its will and distorts everything it encounters." Years ago, Dr. Glenn Loury objected to a strategy of portraying blacks as victims: "the first axiom to the credo of racial loyalty is that when blacks fail, it is whites who are responsible."[ccliii]

Dr. John McWhorter commenting on the book White Fragility said: "In 2020—as opposed to 1920—I neither need nor want anyone to muse on how whiteness privileges them over me. Nor do I need wider society to undergo teachings in how to be exquisitely sensitive about my feelings. I see no connection between DiAngelo's brand of reeducation and vigorous, constructive activism in the real world on issues of import to the Black community. And I cannot imagine that any Black readers

---

[137] Ali was born in Somalia and later lived in Saudi Arabia and the Netherlands, before becoming an American citizen.

could willingly submit themselves to DiAngelo's ideas while considering themselves adults of ordinary self-regard and strength. Few books about race have more openly infantilized Black people than this supposedly authoritative tome."[ccliv]

The Economist also discussed the problem of developing discriminatory race-based programs to solve issues of discrimination. They argued that tackling discrimination is best served with economic programs that strive to give all disadvantaged people assistance to increase their skills and consequently incomes and all the good that this can bring. A very definite non-benevolently anti-racist strategy and one aligned with the censored opponents. They further drew attention to the consequences of exacerbating divisions between blacks and non-blacks, for example, by calling non-blacks racists. [cclv] They seemed to be talking out of turn.

### The new diagnosis may cause progress to stagnate

The new diagnosis that blacks suffer from inequality of opportunity driven by systemic racism has received so much support. Plenty of funds have been and will continue to be allocated or shifted to programs to address the systemic racist narrative. So much support would seem to ensure success, except that unopposed narratives are often untrue, like this one. In this case, widespread support could cause anti-racist progress to stagnate.

Being falsely accused of being a racist is a venomous accusation. It's analogous to the worst of racial slurs. Worse, in the current environment refuting it has been impossible. The environment has become similar to #MeToo where all women were to be believed and alleged culprits disbelieved. #MeToo offered valuable lessons in how not to address discrimination. Women were believed: men were sexist pigs. Not some men - all men. Men that were in a position to help women advance, retreated and it wasn't because they were sexist. Women had to learn the hard way that they needed men to advance and there were better ways to address discrimination than a public beheading. Presenting whites as a giant KKK is likely to have a similar result.

BLM has a name that has captured the attention of people all over the world, but if the objective is anti-racism, some BLM positions will backfire. BLM's call to de-emphasize the nuclear family is a recipe for greater income inequality and discrimination. It is also anti-American, so is promoting anything communist/Marxist, and calls to defund the police. American freedoms rely on rule of law and this relies on effective policing. People espousing any of these views will face bias and it doesn't matter what color they are. [138]

It's also not helpful that the movement is specifically for blacks (and Native Americans[139] and LGBTQ). For decades, the term people of color (POC) has been used to present a united block of non-white ethnicities.

[138] Some have speculated that BLM investors bothered by these aspects of their platform led in late 2020 to removing the destruction of the nuclear family as a key belief on its website. At a similar time, they stopped referring to their supporters as comrades, a popular reference used for fellow communists.

[139] In 2007 the Cherokee Nation in Oklahoma tried to deny the descendants of black slaves' citizenship in their nation. In 2017 a judge ruled that targeting blacks was illegal.

Minimally united in their opposition to whites. Now, black lives have been presented as mattering more than other lives. At the same time, a new acronym BIPOC emphasizes the B in POC and accentuates the exclusion of whites. That may be the point, but governments that fund programs for black or BIPOC communities are unconstitutional and racist because disadvantaged people come in all colors. These programs naturally generate bias.[cclvi]

The media has erred too by downplaying the instances of riots. The media created a steady drumbeat of "mostly peaceful BLM protests," and they were mostly peaceful, but riots were plentiful. In the summer of 2020, there were 557 riots involving BLM activists.[cclvii] Most Americans supported the peaceful protests, but most Americans did not support the rioting and looting, and they abhorred attacks on the police. "There is a long tradition of rule of law in the United States." It would be impossible to have a nation rich with protected freedoms, like the United States, without rule of law. If people disrespected the law, "the streets in your community would quickly become a chaotic and less safe place. Police officers might be overwhelmed trying to help the situation, or ignored altogether."[cclviii] Prophetic. That's from 1998.

Dissing the rule of law with violence and looting was cementing the stereotype of blacks as dangerous, law breakers, and anti-American. An increase in unconscious biases is inevitable when protesters use violence, and when they are seen as anti-America or anti-American.[cclix] Many drew attention to rioters as diverse, which didn't weaken the impact on the black stereotype. These were BLM activists and "protests."

Professional sports, Hollywood, and the media will continue to raise awareness to social injustice. Awareness will have limited near-term effect. Dr. Thomas Pettigrew from the University of California, Santa Cruz researched prejudice for more than fifty years. He showed how difficult it can be for people to eliminate prejudices that were formed early in life, even when people are determined to eliminate them.[cclx] JFK was ahead of his time when he said, "[Discrimination] must be solved in the homes of every American in every community across our country."

The current environment will cause progress to stagnate for other reasons. The 7x24 attention to blacks being surrounded by racists and racism will lead to unintended consequences. It creates an environment where blacks will be more pessimistic and understate progress, and it will increase perceptions of racism. Blacks will be inclined to believe the narrative that racism is everywhere. No question blacks perceive more discrimination than whites do for blacks, much as women perceive more discrimination than men do for women. Do perceptions match reality? In 2020, a group of young BLM supporters were asked how many unarmed black men had been killed by police in 2019. The estimates were 1000-1400. The answer was 9. [cclxi] In 2017, the Robert Wood Johnson Foundation found that while 92% of African Americans believe they face discrimination, only 32% have said they have experienced it in health care, which is regularly cited as being rife with racism.[140,141] In this study, there were also higher beliefs about perceived vs experienced discrimination with Latino-Americans and Asian-Americans. One

---

[140] Reports of experiencing discrimination are also perceptions.
[141] Whites also believe they face discrimination, but few pinpoint experiences.

reason perceptions often do not match reality is because "research suggests that minorities may less often than majorities view contact situations as involving equal status."[cclxii] Perceiving inequality is perceiving discrimination, but that does not make it so.

Another reason perceptions don't match reality is because people are fed a steady diet of half-truths. On any given day there will be another article on the disproportionate number of blacks in different professions, or out of work. The implications are that the reason is racism. But the articles never address if blacks have the same qualifications in terms of educational degrees or experiences, if they live in areas with lots of jobs, or if they even applied. A lack of qualifications is the number one reason people don't attain different jobs. But a sedentary somebody that doesn't live in an area with job opportunities has a 100% chance of not having the same opportunities as someone that does. These are non-discriminatory reasons for not having the same opportunities. When these details are left out, perceptions of racism will naturally but wrongly increase.

Anyone in America watching the steady diet of defunding the police initiatives would be surprised at this disjointed thread because it doesn't fit the perception of legions of racist cops.

- Blacks are 33% to 100% more likely than other ethnicities to have received help from a police officer that helped keep them safe in a potentially dangerous situation.
  Monmouth poll, June 2, 2020.
- "We know that police don't keep us safe — and as long as we continue to pump money into our corrupt criminal justice system at the expense of housing, health, and education investments — we will never be truly safe
  Black Lives Matter, July 6, 2020.
- 81% of Black Americans Don't Want Less Police Presence Despite Protests— Some Want More Cops: Poll.
  Newsweek, August 5, 2020.[cclxiii]

Perceptions of discrimination are ripe for inaccuracies because up to 90% of biases are unconscious.[cclxiv] Unconscious biases are very hard to concretely detect and measure and they can be perceived more frequently by people that believe they are doomed to discrimination, populations with histories of discrimination, those that believe they are surrounded by racists, and those that have experienced or perceived discrimination. Perceptions can be influenced by strong identification with an ingroup. African-Americans more than any racial group find the identity of their race extremely important.[cclxv, cclxvi] A strong black identity is seen as healthy and identifying with another group is seen as unhealthy.[cclxvii] Blacks are glorified, and whites denigrated.[cclxviii] This really increases the chance that perceptions will diverge from reality, but they can be embraced and defended as reality. They can affect psychological development.[cclxix] "For members of disadvantaged groups, attributions to prejudice are likely to be internal, stable, uncontrollable, and convey widespread exclusion and devaluation of one's group."[cclxx]

There is another downside of having a strong in-group identity. This has shown to be a significant generator of unconscious bias against others outside the group.[cclxxi]

Perceptions of discrimination feed more perceptions of discrimination. A young non-white person that perceives bias due to her race can inadvertently create a foundation for regularly perceiving discrimination. During a 2020 peaceful BLM counter protest in support of police a sixteen-year-old black girl called the sight of mostly white protesters sad. "Black people are dying, and they are defending the ones killing them."[cclxxii] How could a girl this young think this? She surely did not know that her comment was very misguided. She could not have known that unarmed blacks are no more likely to die at the hands of white police officers than unarmed whites, or that black officers are more likely to kill unarmed whites than white officers.[cclxxiii,142] What chance does this young lady have of not perceiving racism everywhere she goes even without the steady drumbeat of racist America?

The current environment of newly woke people supporting social justice will cause progress for blacks to stagnate for another reason. "Each day, college-educated millennials race to social media to practice the rituals of wokeness by condemning various cultural artifacts as racist and policing the discourse. Statues are coming down, and the "b" in black is being capitalized. Corporations, private schools, and major philanthropic organizations are declaring that "black lives matter." …Elite institutions have committed themselves to a theory, program, and performance increasingly detached from the aspirations, worldviews, and everyday concerns of millions of blacks."[cclxxiv]

President Obama was in tune with everyday concerns: poverty, crime, jobs, kids dropping out of school, ending up in prison, or becoming teen parents. Concerns that would logically rise with a 30% increase in black children being raised without a father since 2008 and a preference for self-segregation over integration. But these concerns are being sidelined by the misdiagnosis of America as a land of racists.

### America the Anti-racist leader

In a series of studies with biased people in 2016, people showed pro-black biases to give black candidates an edge.[cclxxv] In a 2001 study, managers that ostensibly were biased against black people, were more likely to hire blacks.[cclxxvi] These studies are supportive of American organizational leaders endeavoring to create level playing fields for all employees. Their actions exceed anything the government could ask for. In 2017 Deloitte found that 66% of CEOs in the United States see diversity as an important issue. In the midst of Black Lives Matter protests, corporations all over America began announcing new programs, commitments and donations in support of increasing opportunities for blacks. Blacks, more than any other racial group, see a benefit in programs that consider race.[cclxxvii] Obviously, not because America is a racist society. Many corporations were in agreement with focusing specifically on blacks, but they had to contend with racial preferences being illegal in the United States. They can't prefer Asians, whites, Latinos or blacks. Since the middle of the 20th century, American corporations have played a weighty role ensuring that their employment practices

---

[42] The study also showed that blacks and Latinos were more likely to experience non-lethal force by police, but a direct correlation to race rather than other factors could not be determined.

treat all people equally. They are a primary enforcement arm of the government's anti-discrimination laws.

Corporate commitments to diversity and inclusion have been in place for decades and it has grown stronger as: employers recognize the value workforces and the American public place on diversity, executives recognize the productivity gains of diverse teams, and CEOs see their roles as catalysts for change.[cclxxviii] This includes more and more black CEOs and other black executives. In 2012 the magazine Black Enterprise featured 100 of the most powerful blacks in industry, in 2017 they changed this to be the 300 most powerful.

One challenge CEOs leading diversity and inclusion initiatives have faced is that more diversity means more unconscious discrimination. Unconscious bias and racial sensitivity training have become the answer. The problem is it's rarely effective. People have carried stereotype thumbprints in their brains for years and decades and it's not going to change with training. Not changing might seem like a good outcome because this type of training can also increase biases. One of the most powerful reasons this occurs is that people are offended that they are thought to be racists (or sexists). Why else are they attending the training?

Neutralizing unconscious biases is complicated but there are plenty of investments in researching and developing alternative solutions. Are there any technologies or training that can change how people think? Or that can counteract their upbringings and experiences in life? That is unclear, but this has not been stopping Americans from trying to exorcise discriminatory thoughts that could lead to discriminatory actions. While this is taking place, it's important to remember that biases result in discriminatory actions about 4% of the time.[cclxxix]

Discrimination, discrimination, discrimination. Today, every racial group in America complains about discrimination, even Asians, the highest paid and most educated. Women complain too. It's a problem the world over. Minorities and women face discrimination. What's different in America is that for seventy-five years it has and continues to be addressed, it is decreasing and there are tangible signs everywhere. The pace of progress is faster than anywhere in the world, but everyone is dissatisfied with the pace. People want a magic wand to deliver equality now. If only we weren't humans and could rebuild history from scratch.

There are some ways that might speed up progress. First the false narratives of whites as racists and America as systemically racist has to end. Progress isn't made when problems are misdiagnosed. Besides this is causing some people to perceive racism everywhere and others to find comfort with like people. These are outcomes that discourage integration or even mingling with diverse groups. Next, it's important to refresh our memories on why America has been held up as the model for multiracial societies. It's integration -- not multiculturalism. Separate but equal does not work. Finally, we need to make sure time and money are invested in programs that prepare people for better opportunities, rather than benevolently racist programs that solidify subordination. When a program discourages people from moving to find better work, getting a better education, or co-parenting, this is a program that will solidify subordination.

While America has been embroiled in a one-sided discussion of discrimination, in other parts of the world the topic has been censored. Instead, nations with highly discriminatory societies like China, Russia, and Iran have piled on to degrade racism in America that seems so evident in free-speech America's non-stop narrative of systemically racist America. During BLM protests Iran's foreign minister lambasted America: "the voices of the protesters must be heard." In November 2019 at least 304 unarmed Iranian protesters were killed and thousands arbitrarily detained.[cclxxx]

Discriminated people all over the world, like many Iranians, could only hope that their nations would end censorship and give them a voice that might inspire action. In Africa, the Voice of America reported that descendants of slaves wondered how there could be more equality between blacks and whites in America than between blacks in Africa. [cclxxxi] Too bad it wasn't the Voice of Nigeria reporting.

There have also been leaders of western nations and some in Latam saying we don't have racism like the United States. In many cases, free presses corrected the score. It would be nice if more of America's free presses corrected the score. America is not a systemically racist nation. It can lay a claim to being the first nation to put in place a system of anti-racism, and it has remained the leading anti-racist nation. In 1945 America set in motion a movement to end discrimination all over the world. Since this time, it has passed more laws, has had more private and public sector initiatives to level the playing field, and attracts more diverse immigrants annually than any other country. Signs of success in terms of increasing numbers of professionals, legislators, and leaders, and rising income and educational levels for all of its minorities are everywhere.

The acceptance and perpetuation of an erroneous systemic racist claim is because people don't know what America's commitment to anti-racism has achieved, and they obviously have no idea what a systemically racist society looks like. If they wanted to know, there are plenty of nations to choose from, for example, China, India, Iran, Saudi Arabia, Liberia, and Malaysia. Here they can see what racism looks like when its baked into national systems of government and into society.

Discrimination was not supposed to be part of American society. America's Declaration of Independence (1776) said, "we hold these truths to be self-evident that all men are created equal." What did that mean in 1776? Probably not what it is taken to mean today, but it has become an ideal that since 1945, the country has made demonstrable progress toward achieving. Martin Luther King's dream that one day this nation will hold these truths to be self-evident is also the dream of America and Americans of every color and creed.

A nation with such a dream in a world where nations commonly conceal or deny histories of discrimination, censor minority views, arbitrarily imprison minorities, are blind to discrimination or see it as a useful way to maintain order and privilege is quite extraordinary. But this is America.

# Conclusion

Before 1945, populations all over the world were legally stratified. Discriminating against some groups was seen as natural – a way to order society. Nineteen forty-five ushered in a new zeitgeist. No more legal discrimination; diverse populations were to have equal fundamental freedoms. This notion was universally applauded and every nation affixed its signature to the UN Charter to confirm its' commitment. An epidemic of excuses followed.

Highly discriminatory practices before 1945 continued. In most successor states of Islamic empires populations have been officially or unofficially stratified by religion. Those following the official religion are superior and others inferior. The Chinese Empire saw non-Chinese as inferior; China still does. It also sees Chinese that have not assimilated as inferior and something that requires remedial action. In China, assimilation does not mean fundamental freedoms for all. Indeed, these freedoms conflict with social order. Order, not freedom, is the priority. The Russian Empire was partial to followers of Eastern Orthodox Christianity, and so is Russia. Russia is actually partial to white, straight, males, that follow Eastern Orthodoxy and are ethnically Slavic Russians.

Will these nations ever prioritize delivering fundamental freedoms to all people? Order is the priority – not freedom. This priority is evident in their governments; they are autocracies.[143] Autocracies strive for control. Freedoms conflict with control. Should minorities, or anyone object to discriminatory treatment, they can discover there is no fundamental freedoms for free speech or arbitrary actions of the state.

Protecting fundamental freedoms for all is also not universally embraced in sub-Saharan Africa, South Asia, or Latam. Historical patterns of discrimination, some hereditary, and including slavery, social hierarchies, and indentured servitude continue to be practiced. Making populations statelessness is new.

Since 1945, the greatest progress toward achieving a commitment to fundamental freedoms for all has been in the western nations. Here legal systems have been created to eliminate systemic racism, and there have been many initiatives to level the playing fields. The challenges these nations continue to face have been numerous, particularly because they have simultaneously permitted the introduction of more diversity. Additional discrimination naturally follows. Many western nations with a historical partiality toward white homogenous populations are actually new to diversity and consequently the discriminatory challenges in democratic societies. These nations know, or they are learning firsthand how complex it is to keep people of all races, religions, and ethnicities content with the realities of multiracial nations. This is so even with governments and private sector institutions endeavoring to deliver fair and equitable societies. This is because institutions alone cannot end discrimination. US President John F. Kennedy knew this early on. "[Discrimination] must be solved in the homes of every [person] in every community across [every] country."

---

[143] Democracy requires a lot more than hosting elections.

It actually requires more than parents. Democratic governments cannot stop journalists, commentators, teachers and different leaders that purposely or inadvertently teach and reinforce discrimination. They cannot force children to go to school, or parents to live together. They cannot address perceptions of discrimination that deviate from reality, or most unconscious biases. They cannot force people to behave in a manner that will likely reduce discrimination, they cannot cancel history, and they cannot halt discriminatory beliefs rooted in history and reinforced at home, school, the media, communities, or generally in society.

Getting from societies where discrimination was natural to societies where there is equality of opportunity is a mammoth change. A change most have shown no interest in making. For nations committed to anti-racism, there are no quick fixes. The best that can be hoped for is steady forward progress.

# Appendix – Countries by Region

Note: Territories are distinguished by noting the parent nation in parenthesis, for example, Anguilla (UK).

**Central Asia**
Abkhazia (unrecognized by the UN)
Armenia
Azerbaijan
Georgia
Kazakhstan
Kyrgyzstan
South Ossetia (unrecognized by the UN)
Turkmenistan
Tajikistan
Uzbekistan

**Central Europe**
Bosnia and Herzegovina
Albania
Bulgaria
Croatia
Czech Republic
Estonia
Hungary
Kosovo (unrecognized by UN)
Latvia
Lithuania
Macedonia
Montenegro
Poland
Romania
Serbia
Slovak Republic
Slovenia

**Eastern Asia**
China
Hong Kong, SAR of China
Japan
Macau, SAR of China
Mongolia
North Korea
South Korea
Taiwan (unrecognized by the UN)

**Eastern Europe**
Belarus
Moldova
Russia
Ukraine

**English-Speaking North America**
Divided by the Mainland and the island countries in the Caribbean.
**Mainland**
Canada
United States
**The Caribbean** Anguilla (UK) Antigua and Barbuda
Aruba (NL)
Barbados
Bermuda
British Virgin Islands (UK)
Cayman Islands (UK)
Curacao (NL)
Dominica
Grenada
Haiti
Jamaica
Montserrat (UK)
Puerto Rico (US)
Saba (NL)
St. Barthelemy
St. Kitts and Nevis
St. Lucia
Saint Martin/Sint Maarten (FR and NL)
St. Vincent and the Grenadines
Trinidad and Tobago
Turks and Caicos Islands (UK)
US Virgin Islands (US)

**Latin America (Latam).** Divided into Mexico, Central America,
South America and the Caribbean.
**Mexico**
**Central America**
Belize
Costa Rica
Guatemala
Honduras
Nicaragua Panama
**South America**
Argentina
Bolivia
Brazil Chile
Ecuador
French Guiana (FR)
Guyana
Paraguay
Peru
Surinam Uruguay
Venezuela

**Caribbean**
Cuba
The Dominican Republic
Guadeloupe (FR)
Haiti
Martinique (FR)

**The Middle East and North Africa**
**Middle East**
Iran
Iraq
Israel
Jordon
Kuwait
Lebanon
Oman
Palestinian territories (UN permanent observer)
Qatar
Saudi Arabia
Syria
Turkey
United Arab Emirates
Yemen
**North Africa** Algeria
Djibouti
Egypt
Libya
Mauritania
Morocco
Sudan
Tunisia
Western Sahara (disputed territory of Morocco)

**Oceania** (Only inhabited islands.)
American Samoa (US)
Australia
Cook Islands (NZ)
French Polynesia (FR)
Fiji
Guam (US)
Kiribati Islands
Northern Mariana Islands (US)
Marshall Islands
Micronesia (the Federated States of)
Nauru
New Caledonia (FR)
New Zealand
Niue (NZ)
Norfolk Island (AU)
Palau
Pitcairn Islands (UK)

**Oceania continued**
Papua New Guinea
Samoa
Solomon Islands
Tokelau (NZ)
Tonga
Tuvalu
Vanuatu
Wallis and Futuna (FR)

**Southeast Asia**
Brunei
Cambodia
East Timor/Timor Leste
Indonesia
Laos
Malaysia
Myanmar
Philippines
Singapore
Thailand Vietnam

**South Asia**
Afghanistan
Bangladesh
Bhutan
India
Nepal
Maldives
Pakistan
Sri Lanka

**Sub-Saharan Africa.** Divided by geographic region.
**West**
Benin
Burkina Faso
Cape Verde
Côte d'Ivoire (Ivory Coast)
The Gambia
Ghana
Guinea
Guinea-Bissau
Liberia
Mali
Niger
Nigeria
Senegal
Sierra Leone Togo

**Sub-Saharan Africa (East) continued**
**East**
Burundi
Comoros
Eritrea
Ethiopia
Kenya
Madagascar
Malawi
Mauritius
Mayotte (FR)
Mozambique
Réunion (FR)
Rwanda
Seychelles
Somalia
South Sudan
Tanzania
Uganda
Zambia
Zimbabwe
**Middle**
Angola
Cameroon
The Central African Republic
Chad
Republic of the Congo
Equatorial Guinea
Gabon
Republic of the Congo
São Tomé and Príncipe
**South**
Botswana
Eswatini (Renamed in 2018. Formerly Swaziland.)
Lesotho
Namibia
Saint Helena (UK)
South Africa

**Western Europe**
Aland (FI)
Andorra
Austria
Belgium
Cyprus
Denmark
Faroe Islands (DK)
Finland
France
Germany
Gibraltar (UK)
Greece
Greenland (DK)
Guernsey (UK)
Iceland
Ireland
Isle of Man (UK)
Italy
Jersey (UK)
Luxembourg
Lichtenstein
Malta
Monaco
The Netherlands
Norway
Portugal
San Marino
Spain
Sweden
Switzerland
Turkish Republic of Northern Cyprus (unrecognized by the UN)
United Kingdom (England, Northern Ireland, Scotland, Wales)
Vatican City (UN permanent observer)

# References

[i] Historical Survey – Slave Owning Societies. Encyclopedia Britannica. Retrieved July 24, 2020.

[ii] Rodzinski, Witold. A History of China. Pergamon Press, 1979.

[iii] Chang, Jung, Halliday, Joe. Mao: The Unknown Story. Jonathan Cape, London, 2005.

[iv] "China's Crusade Against the Muslims of East Turkestan (Xinjiang)." The Khilafah, July 7, 2009.

[v] Xu, Vicky, Cave, Danielle, Leibold, James, Munro, Kelsey, Ruse, Nathan. Uyghurs for Sale. Australian Strategic Policy Institute, 2019.

[vi] "Tibet profile-Overview." BBC.com., November 13, 2014

[vii] Goldberg, Jonah. We Shouldn't Ignore Systemic Discrimination in China. The National Review, August 22, 2018.

[viii] Linzhu, Wang. The Identification of Minorities in China. Asia-Pacific Law and Policy Journal, Vol 16:2, 2015.

[ix] Hsiao-Hung Pai. "China's rural migrant workers deserve more respect from the city-dwellers." The Guardian, August 25, 2012.

[x] Prison Slaves. Al Jazeera, March 25, 2012.

[xi] Girard, Bonnie. "Racism is Alive and Well in China." The Diplomat, April 23, 2020.

[xii] Wesby, Maya. "Japan's Problem with Race." Newsweek, August 19, 2015.

[xiii] Stokes, Bruce. Hostile Neighbors: China vs. Japan. Pew Research, September 13, 2016

[xiv] Logan, Nick. "Examples of North Korea human rights violations from UN report." Globalnews.ca, February 18, 2014

[xv] Yang, Jiayun. China's plan to relax immigration rules spurs all sorts of hateful comments from nationalistic Chinese. Supchina.com, March 6, 2020.

[xvi] Serfes, Nektarios. "In Memory of the 50 Million Victims of The Orthodox Christian Holocaust." Serfes.Org, October 1999.

[xvii] Lai, K. S. Growth of Muslim Population in Medieval India (A. D. 1000–1800). Delhi: Research Publications, 1973. xi. Ferishta, Muhammad Qasim Hindu Shah Astarabadi and Jonathan Scott. Firishta's History of Dekkan. (Vol 1). Jonathan Scott, translator, London: John Stockdale, 1794.

[xviii] Elst, Koonraed. "India's Holocaust." HinduismToday.com, March 1999. xiii. Montalbano, William. "Israel Troubled by Jews 'Dropout' Rate." Los Angeles Times, June 2, 1988.

[xix] Durant, Will. "Our Oriental Heritage." First Communications, 1997.

[xx] McHugo, A Concise History of Sunnis & Shi'is. Saqi Books, 2018.

[xxi] Ibid

[xxii] Segal, Ronald. Islam's Black Slaves: The Other Black Diaspora. Farrar, Straus, and Giroux, 2001.

[xxiii] Appleton's Annual Cyclopaedia 1891 and Register of Important Events. New York: D. Appleton, 1892.

[xxiv] "The Arab Muslim Slave Trade of Africa, The Untold Story." Originalpeople.org, November 15, 2012.

[xxv] "'Horrible Traffic in Circassian Women—Infanticide in Turkey.' New York Daily Times, August 6, 1856." Lostmuseum.cuny.edu.

[xxvi] Bostom, A. G. "The Legacy of Jihad: Islamic Holy War and the Fate of Non-Muslims." Prometheus Books, 2005.

[xxvii] Davis, Robert C. Christian Slaves, Muslim Masters: White Slavery in the Mediterranean, the Barbary Coast and Italy, 1500–1800. Palgrave Macmillan, 2003.

[xxviii] Grabmeier, Jeff. Research Reveals Massive Extent of Slavery Between Muslims, Christians For Three Centuries. OSU.edu, March 8, 2010.

[xxix] Clarence-Smith, W. G. (Ed.). The Economics of the Indian Ocean Slave Trade in the Nineteenth Century. Routledge, 1989.

[xxx] "The East African Slave Trade." BBC.co.uk., retrieved April 17, 2018.

[xxxi] Thornton, John. Africa and Africans in the Making of the Atlantic World, 1400–1800.

Cambridge University Press, 1998.

xxxii "And then there were none." The Economist, January 2, 2016.

xxxiii Statistics of Jews. The Bureau of Social Research, 1920.

xxxiv Property of Italians and Jews Confiscated by Libyan Regime. NY Times, July 22, 1970.

xxxv Abbas, Fatin. Coming to Terms with Sudan's history of slavery. African Arguments, January 18, 2015.

xxxvi Viewpoint from Sudan - where black people are called slaves. BBC.com, July 25, 2020.

xxxvii Slavery in Sudan. Cultural Survival.org, September 1988.

xxxviii Sudan accused of making thousands slaves in Darfur. Antislavery.org, January 6, 2009.

xxxix Abrahamian, Ervand. Tortured Confessions. Berkeley: University of California Press, 1999.

xl "Sudan: African Initiative for Pride and Dignity to Honor President Al-Bashir Friday in Addis Ababa." Allafrica.com, July 28, 2016.

xli Antislavery,org, Sudan accused.

xlii Schmid. Alex. Public Opinion Survey Data to Measure Sympathy and Support for Islamist Terrorism: A Look at Muslim Opinions on Al Qaeda and IS. International Centre for Counter-Terrorism, February 2017.

xliii Convert, pay tax, or die, Islamic State warns Christians. Reuters, July 18, 2014.

xliv Lamb, Christina "Khomeini Fatwa Led to Killing 30,000 in Iran." The Telegraph, February 4, 2004.

xlv Maida, Adam. "They are not our Brothers." Human Rights Watch, 2017.

xlvi Hawley, Emily. ISIS Crimes Against the Shia: The Islamic State's Genocide Against Shia Muslims. Genocide Studies International. 11. 160-181, 2018.

xlvii BBC Poll: Israel Among World's Least Popular Nations, Haaretz, May 25, 2013.

xlviii Pinnell, Owen, Kelly, Jess. Slave markets found on Instagram and other apps. BBC.com, October 13, 2019.

xlix As slave trade abolition is celebrated, millions of Africans continue to live as slaves. Dw.com, retrieved August 13, 2020.

Hosking, Geoffrey. Russia, People and Empire. Harvard University Press, 1997.

i Lowe, Heinz-Dietrich. "Russian Nationalism and Tsarist Nationalities Policies in Semi-Constitutional Russia, 1905–1914." The University of Heidelberg, retrieved December 20, 2018.

ii Forbes, Ethan, Suzanne Lauer, Kathleen Koonz, and Pam Sweeney. "A Resource Guide for Teachers: Russian Jewish Immigration 1880–1920." FitchburgState.edu, retrieved December 20, 2018.

iii Applebaum, Anne. Applebaum, Gulag: A History, p. xvii. Random House, 2003.

v Applebaum, Anne. Red Famine: Stalin's War on Ukraine. Doubleday, 2017.

vi "Holodomor 1932–1933." Holodomorct.org. Retrieved December 20, 2018.

viii Allworth, Edward, A. Central Asia. Duke University Press, 1995.

ix Snyder, Timothy. Bloodlands: Europe Between Hitler and Stalin. Vintage, 2010

x Magocsi, Paul R. A History of Ukraine: The Land and its Peoples. University of Toronto Press, 1996.

xi Arnold, R. Systematic racist violence in Russia between 'hate crime' and 'ethnic conflict.' Theoretical Criminology, 19(2), 239–256, 2015

xii Gould, Stephen Jay. The Mismeasure of Man. W. W. Norton, 1996.

xiii Arnold, Systematic racist violence.

xiv Buchanan, Joe. Are you happy to cheat us? Human Rights Watch, 2009.

xv Open Society. Ethnic Profiling in the Moscow Metro. New York: Open Society Institute, 2006.

xvi Why are German neo-Nazis training in Russia? Dw.com, retrieved August 3, 2020.

xvii The new Jews. The Economist, February 17, 2005.

[lxviii] Herbert, David. A Different Dynamic? Explaining Prejudice Against Muslims in the Russian Federation: Islamophobia or Internalised Racial Hierarchy? in: Connections. A Journal for Historians and Area Specialists, 2019.

[lxix] Lopatina S., Kostenko V, Ponarin E. National Pride and Individual-Choice Attitudes in Ten Post-Soviet Countries. The Journal of Sociology and Social Anthropology], 22(4): 166–201, 2019.

[lxx] Constable, Olivia, Remie. Trade and Traders in Muslim Spain. Cambridge University Press, 2008.

[lxxi] Ryan, Edward. "Spanish Inquisition." Encyclopedia Britannica, retrieved April 6, 2018.

[lxxii] Wheat, David. "Iberian Roots of the Transatlantic Slave Trade, 1440–1640." The Gilder Lehrman Institute of American History, retrieved October 15, 2017.

[lxxiii] Carreira. A. The African Slave Trade from the Fifteenth to the Nineteenth Century. UNESCO, 1978.

[lxxiv] Snyder, Timothy. "The Reich's Forgotten Atrocity." The Guardian, October 21, 2010

[lxxv] "Axis Invasion of Yugoslavia." The United States Holocaust Museum, 2016.

[lxxvi] Judt, Tony. Postwar: A History of Europe since 1945. New York: The Penguin Press, 2005.

[lxxvii] Gerstenfeld, Manfred. Tens of Millions of Europeans Have Demonic Views of Israel. The Began-Sadat Center for Strategic Studies, March 20, 2020

[lxxviii] Abdelkader, Engy. A Comparative Analysis of European Islamophobia: France, UK, Germany, Netherlands, and Sweden, UCLA: Journal of Islamic and Near Eastern Law, 2017.

[lxxix] Neufield, Jeremy. Do Muslim immigrants assimilate? Niskanecenter.org, April 3, 2017.

[lxxx] Bulman, May. "Brexit: People voted to leave EU because they feared immigration, major survey finds." The Independent, June 17, 2017.

[lxxxi] Jersey, Ted. "UK entering 'unchartered territory' of Islamophobia after Brexit vote." The Independent, June 27, 2016.

[lxxxii] Beckford, Martin. "Muslims in UK top 3 million for first time." Daily Mail, January 30, 2016

[lxxxiii] Schmid. Alex. Public Opinion Survey Data to Measure Sympathy and Support for Islamist Terrorism: A Look at Muslim Opinions on Al Qaeda and IS. International Centre for Counter-Terrorism, February 2017.

[lxxxiv] Simpson, B., Willer, R., & Feinberg, M. Does Violent Protest Backfire? Testing a Theory of Public Reactions to Activist Violence. Socius, 2018.

[lxxxv] Younge, Gary. Waking up to the realities of racism in the UK. Financial Times, June 26, 2020.

[lxxxvi] Quillan, Lincoln, Heath, Anthony, Pager, Devah, Mitdboen, Arnfinn, AU- Fleishman, Fenella, Hexel, Ole. et al. Do Some Countries Discriminate More than Others? Evidence from 97 Field Experiments of Racial Discrimination in Hiring. Sociological Science, June 2019.

[lxxxvii] Ames, Paul. Portugal confronts its slave trade past. Politico.eu, February 12, 2018.

[lxxxviii] Olusoga, David. The history of British slave ownership has been buried; now its scale can be revealed. The Guardian, July 11, 2015.

[lxxxix] Cartwright, Mark. Serfs. Ancient History Encyclopedia, December 2018.

[xc] Noack, Rick. "Angela Merkel: German Chancellor says multiculturalism is a sham." The Independent, December 14, 2015.

[xci] Miers, Suzanne. "Twentieth Century Solutions to the Abolition of Slavery." Yale.edu, retrieved May 1, 2018

[xcii] Liberia: The End of 'State-Sanctioned' Discrimination? FrontpageAfricaonline, January 29, 2018.

[xciii] International Commission of Enquiry in Liberia. Report of the International Commission of Inquiry into the Existence of Slavery and Forced Labor in the Republic of Liberia: Monrovia, Liberia, September 8, 1930. Washington: Govt. Print. Off., 1931. United States Department of State..

[xciv] Renee C. Redman, The League of Nations and the Right to be Free from Enslavement: The First Human Right to Be Recognized as Customary International Law - Freedom: Beyond the United States, 70 Chi.-Kent L. Rev. 759, 1994.

xcv Santana, Genesys. A case of double consciousness, americo-liberians and indigenous liberian relations 1840-1930. University of Central Florida, 2012.

xcvi Mathews, Martin, P. "Nigeria: A Country Study." Nova Science Publishers, 2002.

xcvii Slavery among the Igbo. American Historical Society, historians.org. retrieved July 23, 2020.

xcviii 'My Nigerian great-grandfather sold slaves.' BBC.com, July 16, 2020.

xcix Nwaubani, A.T. The Descendants of Slaves in Nigeria Fight for Equality. The New Yorker, July 19, 2019.

c Nwaubani, A.T. The Descendants of Slaves, 2019.

ci Discrimination based on descent in Africa. The International Dalit Solidarity Network, retrieved August 13, 2020.

cii Nigeria's Slave Descendants Hope Race Protests Help End Discrimination. VOAnews.com, June 29, 2020.

ciii McGowan, Patrick. "Coups and Conflicts in West Africa, 1955-2004." Armed Forces and Society, October 1, 2005

civ Armed Conflict Location & Event Data Project. Retrieved January 6, 2017.

cv How well has Rwanda healed 25 years after the genocide? The Economist, March 28, 2019.

cvi Watts, Jonathan. Maasai herders driven off land to make way for luxury safaris, report says. The Guardian, May 10, 2018.

cvii Pygmies want UN tribunal to address cannibalism. The Sydney Morning Herald, 2003.

cviii Merciless Plight of African Pygmies. Cultural Survival, retrieved July 21, 2020.

cix The Bushmen. Survival International, retrieved July 21, 2020.

cx Meredith, Martin. "The Fate of Africa." Public Affairs, 2005.

cxi Brink, Eugene, Mulder, Connie. How the response to black and white racism differs – Solidarity. Solidarity Research Institute, April 5, 2017.

cxii Wike, R., Stokes, B., Simmons, K. Negative views of minorities, refugees common in EU. Pew Research, July 11, 2016.

cxiii Shanahan, Rodger. Malaysia and its Shi'a "Problem." Middle East Institute, July 25, 2014.

cxiv Qureshi, H. M. Z. Muslim Revivalism in 19th Century India. Oxford: St. Cross College, 2015.

cxv Bangladesh Genocide Archive. Genocidebangladesh.org, retrieved November 30, 2020.

cxvi Boissoneault, Lorraine. The Genocide the U.S. Can't Remember, But Bangladesh Can't Forget. Smithsonian Magazine, December 16, 2016.

cxvii "Bangladesh and Pakistan: The Forgotten War." Time, August 2, 1971.

cxviii "The Hindu Genocide that Hindus and the World Forgot." India Times, retrieved June 7, 2013.

cxix Hindu Human Rights in Bhutan: Excerpts from the HAF 2011 Report. Hindu America Foundation, retrieved September 7, 2016.

cxx Religious discrimination continues in Pakistan amid COVID-19 outbreak; Hindus denied food supplies in Karachi. Timesnownews.com, March 30, 2020.

cxxi Jinnah, Muhammad Ali. Policy speech, November 11, 1947.

cxxii Kumar, Ruchi. "The decline of Afghanistan's Hindu and Sikh communities." Al Jazeera, January 1, 2017.

cxxiii Hucal, Sarah. "Afghanistan: Who are the Hazaras?"Al Jazeera, June 27, 2016.

cxxiv Maley, William. On the Return of Hazaras to Afghanistan. Australian National University, March 4, 2020.

cxxv Shia, Hazaras. European Asylum Office, July 29, 2020.

cxxvi Maldives placed back on US human trafficking watch list. Maldives Independent, July 28, 2015.

cxxvii Braudel, Fernand. "A History of Civilizations." Penguin Books, 1995.

cxxviii Harris, Gardner, "For India's Persecuted Muslim Minority, Caution Follows Hindu Party's Victory." NY Times, May 16, 2014.

cxxix "Can anyone stop Narendra Modi?" The Economist, April 5, 2014.

cxxx Majumdar, Samirah. 5 Facts about religion in India. Pew Research, 2018.

cxxxi Ibid.

cxxxii "The Story of ... Smallpox—and other Deadly Eurasian Germs." PBS, retrieved August 10, 2017.

cxxxiii Mettas, Jean. Répertoire des expéditions négrières françaises au XVIIIe siècle. Société française d'histoire d'outre-mer, 1978.

cxxxiv Historical Survey – Slave Owning Societies. Encyclopedia Britannica retrieved July 24, 2020.

cxxxv "Las Castas-Spanish Racial Classifications." Nativeheritageproject.com, June 15, 2013.

cxxxvi Abbott, Elizabeth. Haiti: A Shattered Nation. Penguin, 2011.

cxxxvii Ribbe, Claude. Napoleon's Crimes. Oneworld Publications, 2005. vi. Hayes, Carlton J. H. "From Nationalism to Imperialism." Panarchy.com, retrieved May 14, 2018.

cxxxviii The Post-Revolutionary Period: 1804–1820. Retrieved May 5, 2017.

cxxxix Nicholls, David. From Dessalines to Duvalier: Race, Colour and National Independence in Haiti. Rutgers University Press, 1979.

cxl Meagher, Arnold. The Coolie Trade. Xlibris, 2008.

cxli Andrew, George Reed. Afro-Latin America. Oxford University Press, 2004.

cxlii Hooker, Juliet. "Indigenous inclusion/black exclusion: Race, ethnicity and multicultural citizenship in Latin America." Journal of Latin American Studies 37(2): 285-310, 2005.

cxliii Hernandez, Tanya Kateri, Afrodescendants, Law, and Race in Latin America. Book Chapter, "Law and Race in Latin America," in Handbook of Law and Society in Latin America, eds. Tatiana Alfonso, Karina Ansolabehere, and Rachel Sieder. Fordham Law Legal Studies Research Paper No. 3589793, 2019.

cxliv Rahier, Jean Muteba. Blackness in the Andes: Ethnographic Vignettes of Cultural Politics in the Time of Multiculturalism. Palgrave Macmillan, 2014.

cxlv Da Costa, Alexandre Emboaba. Reimagining Black Difference and Politics in Brazil: From Racial Democracy to Multiculturalism. Palgrave Macmillan, 2014.

cxlvi Alberto, Paulina, Elena, Eduardo (Eds). Rethinking Race in Modern Argentina. Cambridge University Press, 2016.

cxlvii Guimarães, Antonio Sergio. Preconceito e discriminação: queixas de ofensas e tratamento desigual nos negros no Brasil. Bahia: UFBA Ed. Novos Toques, 1998.

cxlviii Hernández, Tanya Katerí. Racial Subordination in Latin America: The Role of the State, Customary Law, and the New Civil Rights Response. Cambridge University, 2013.

cxlix Escarfuller, Wilda, Frankel, Adam. Racial Apartheid Persists in Latin America. Americas Quarterly, October 13, 2013.

cl Nimatuj, Irma, Ford, Aileen. State of Indigenous People in Land, Territories and Resources in Latin America and the Caribbean. Indigenous People Major Group for Sustainable Development, 2018.

cli Griffiths, Thomas. Indigenous peoples, land tenure and policy in Latin America. Fao.org, retrieved July 28, 2020.

clii "Forced Labour in Latin America." International Labour Office, January 2005.

cliii World Factbook. US Central Intelligence Agency, 2008.

cliv The Return of Populism." The Economist, April 12, 2016.

clv Dornbusch, Rudiger and Sebastian Edwards. The Macroeconomics of Populism in Latin America. University of Chicago Press, 1991.

clvi Katz, J.M. What Happened When a Nation Erased Birthright Citizenship. The Atlantic, November 12, 2018.

clvii Cucolo, Eduardo. Whites Earn 74% More than Blacks in Brazil. Folha de S.Paulo, November 14, 2019.

clviii Long, William, Slavery Ended in 1888: Brazil: No Equality for Blacks Yet. Los Angeles Times, April 9, 1988.

clix Mitchell-Walthour, Gladys. Will Police Forces Undergo Reforms in Latin America. The Dialogue, June 18, 2020.

clx Ramos, Italos. "The Difference Between Black Brazil and Black U.S." Black Agenda Report, October 16, 2007.

clxi Gay, Danielle. The Reality of Indigenous slavery and forced labour in Australia. Vogue, June 14, 2020.

clxii Vayda, Andrew P. "Maori Prisoners and Slaves in the Nineteenth Century." Ethnohistory, vol. 8, no. 2, pp. 144–155, 1961.

clxiii Blundell, Sally. Blackbirding: New Zealand's shameful role in the Pacific Islands slave trade. Noted.co.nz, January 7, 2017.

clxiv Twelve charts on race and racism in Australia. The Conversation, retrieved August 4, 2020.

clxv Gardiner-Garden, John. From Dispossession to Reconciliation. aph.gov.au, 1999.

clxvi Simon-Kumar, Rachel. The Multicultural Dilemma: Amid Rising Diversity and Unsettled Equity Issues, New Zealand Seeks to Address Its Past and Present. Migration Policy Institute, September 5, 2019.

clxvii "Fiji: A Question of Land." BBC, December 11, 2000.

clxviii Tomlins, Christopher. "Reconsidering Indentured Servitude: European Migration and the Early American Labor Force, 1600–1775. Journal of Labor History 42, no.1: 5–43, 2001.

clxix Butler, James Davie. British Convicts Shipped to American Colonies. Oxford Journals. The American Historical Review, 1896.

clxx Butler, British Convicts, 1896.

clxxi Mason, Mary Ann. "Masters and Servants: The American Colonial Model of Child Custody and Control." The International Journal of Children's Rights 2 317–321, 1994.

clxxii "Indentured Servants in the U.S." Pbs.org, retrieved November 16, 2016.

clxxiii From Indentured Servitude to Racial Slavery. PBS.org, retrieved November 26, 2020.

**clxxiv** European Christianity and Slavery. Low Country Digital History Initiative, retrieved November 26, 2020.

clxxv lxii. Gates, Henry Louis. "How Many Slaves Landed in the U.S.?" Pbs.org, retrieved November 16, 2016.

clxxvi Henry, Natasha. Black Enslavement in Canada. The Canadian Encyclopedia, retrieved July 25, 2020.

clxxvii Smith, Ryan. P. How Native American Slaveholders Complicate the Trail of Tears Narrative. The Smithsonian, March 16, 2016.

clxxviii Doran, Michael F. "Negro Slaves of the Five Civilized Tribes." Annals of the Association of American Geographers, vol. 68, no. 3, pp. 335–350, 1978.

clxxix Harper, D. Introduction to Slavery. Slavenorth.com, retrieved July 20, 2020.

clxxx Gates, Henry Lewis. "Did Black People Own Slaves." The Root, 2013.

clxxxi Seybert, Tony. "Slavery and Native Americans in British North America and the United States." SlaveryinAmerica.org, retrieved August 4, 2014.

clxxxii Banner, Stuart. How the Indians Lost their Land. Harvard University Press, 2007

clxxxiii . "German and Irish Immigration." Ushistory.org, retrieved May 3, 2015.

clxxxiv Kierdorf, Douglas. "Getting to know the Know-Nothings. The Boston Globe, January 10, 2016.

clxxxv Data Analysis: African Americans on the Eve of the Civil War. Bowdoin.edu, retrieved July 28, 2020.

clxxxvi Schulman, Marc. Economics and the Civil War. Historycentral.com, retrieved November 26, 2020.

clxxxvii Admin. The Truth About Italian Slaves in America – Padrone Act of 1874. Italian Tribune, July 16, 2020.

clxxxviii Forbes, Ethan, et.al. A Resource Guide for Teachers: Russian Jewish Immigration 1880–1920." Retrieved December 20, 2018.

clxxxix Ford's Anti-Semitism. American Experience, pbs.org, retrieved July 26, 2020.

cxc Yollin, Patricia. A Secret History. The harassment of Italians during World War II has particular relevance today and serves as a warning of what could happen. SF Gate, October 21, 2001.

cxci Cannato, Vincent. What Sets Italian-American immigrants off from other Immigrants. Humanities, Volume 36, Number 1, January/February 2015.

cxcii O'Sullivan, Niamh. Scary tales of New York: life in the Irish slums. New York. The Irish Times, March 23, 2013.

cxciii Wade, Lisa. Irish Apes: Tactics of de-humanization. Society Pages. January 28, 2011.

cxciv Massa, Mark. A Catholic for President: John F. Kennedy and the Secular Theology of the Houston Speech, 1960. Journal of Church and State, 1997.

cxcv Rothman, Joshua. When Bigotry Paraded Through the Streets. The Atlantic, Dec. 4, 2016.

cxcvi Martin, James. Is Anti-Catholicism The Last Acceptable Prejudice? America, March 25, 2000.

cxcvii Fouka, Vasilki, Mazumder, Soumyajit, Tabellini, Marco. From immigrants to Americans: Race and assimilation in the age of mass migration. VoxEU.org, March 27, 2020.

cxcviii Hashik, Scott. Appeals Court Backs Harvard on Affirmative Action. Inside Higher Ed, November 16, 2020.

cxcix Thernstrom, A, Thernstrom, S. Black Progress: How far we've come, and how far we have to go. Brookings.edu., March 1, 1998

cc Black Americans: a profile. Census.gov, 1993.

cci Mills, Barbara Kleban. Predicting Disaster for a Racist America, Louis Farrakhan Envisions an African Homeland for U.S. Blacks. People, September 17, 1990.

ccii Maclay, Kathleen. Obama's race not a factor in election, say economists. Berkeley.edu, February 12, 2009.

cciii Teel, K. S., Verdeli, H., Wickramaratne, P., Warner, V., Vousoura, E., Haroz, E. E., & Talati, A. Impact of a Father Figure's Presence in the Household on Children's Psychiatric Diagnoses and Functioning in Families at High Risk for Depression. Journal of child and family studies, 25(2), 588–597, 2016.

cciv Brown, Jerrod. Father-Absent Homes: Implications for Criminal Justice and Mental Health Professionals." Minnesota Psychological Association, retrieved August 8, 2020.

ccv McLanahan, Sara, Perchesk, Christine. Family Structure and the Reproduction of Inequalities. Office of Population Research, Princeton University, 2008.

ccvi Esposito, Luigi; Romano, Victor Benevolent Racism: Upholding Racial Inequality in the Name of Black Empowerment. The Western Journal of Black Studies, Summer 2014.

ccvii 21.3 % of U.S. Population Participates in Government Assistance Programs Each Month. US Census, May 28, 2015.

ccviii James, Kay. Why we must be bold on welfare reform. Heritage.org, May 12, 2018.

ccix De La Roca, Jorge, Gould Ellen, Ingrid, Steil, Justin. Does Segregation Matter for Latinos? Journal of Housing Economics, 2018.

ccx Special Report- The Midwest: Separate, downtrodden. The Economist, July 25-31, 2020.

ccxi Poorest Cities in the United States, 2011. Neoch.com, retrieved July 31, 2019.

ccxii McCann, Adam. States with Most Racial Progress. Wallethub.com, January 14, 2020.

ccxiii Shambaugh, Jay, Nunn, Ray, Anderson, Stacy. How racial and regional inequality affect economic opportunity. Brookings.edu, February 15, 2019.

ccxiv Fisher, Max. A fascinating map of the world's most and least racially tolerant countries. Washington Post, May 15, 2013.

ccxv Cashin, Sheryll. The Failures of Integration: How Race and Class are Undermining the American Dream. New York: Public Affairs, 2004.

ccxvi Horowitz, Juliana. Americans See Advantages and Challenges in Country's Growing Racial and Ethnic Diversity. Pew Research, May 8, 2019.

ccxvii Chiumenti, Nicholas. Recent Trends in Residential Segregation in New England, Bostonfed.org, April 8, 2020.

ccxviii Residential Segregation Data for U.S. Metro Areas. Governing.com, retrieved August 15, 2020.

ccxix Spader, Jonathan, Rieger, Shannon. Are Integrated Neighborhoods Becoming More Common in the United States. Joint Center for Housing Studies, Harvard University, September 19, 2017.

ccxx Aliprantis. Dionissi. Racial Inequality, Neighborhood Effects, and Moving to Opportunity. Federal Reserve Bank of Cleveland, November 4, 2019.

cxxi Clark, William. Reexamining the Moving to Opportunity Study and its Contribution to Changing the Distribution of Poverty and Ethnic Concentration. National Institute of Health, August 2008.

cxxii Cook, Lindsay. U.S. Education: Still Separate and Unequal. US News, January 28, 2015.

cxxiii Drop out rates. Kidscount Data Center, retrieved August 6, 2020.

cxxiv Educational attainment by race and ethnicity. American Council on Education, retrieved August 5, 2020.

cxxv Myers, Dowell, Pitkin, John. Assimilation Today. American Progress, September 2010.

cxxvi Quillan, Lincoln, et al. Do Some Countries Discriminate More than Others? June 2019.

cxxvii United States. Migration Policy Institute, retrieved, July 27, 2020.

cxxviii Feinup, Matthew. 2020 LDC U.S. Latino GDP Report. California Lutheran University, September 20, 2020.

cxxix Clark, Kevin. The Ten Best States for Black Household Wealth. Black Enterprise, September 19, 2014.

cxxx Anderson, Monica, Lopez, Gustavo. Key Facts about black immigrants in the U.S. Pew Research Center, January 24, 2018.

cxxxi Anderson, Monica. Chapter 1: Statistical Portrait of the U.S. Black Immigrant Population. Pew Research, April 9, 2015.

cxxxii Johnson, Theodore, R. Black-on Black Racism: The Hazards of Implicit bias. The Atlantic, December 26, 2014.

cxxxiii Greenwald, Anthony G et al. "Statistically small effects of the Implicit Association Test can have societally large effects." Journal of Personality and Social Psychology 108 4:553-61, 2015.

cxxxiv Blanton, H., & Jaccard, J. Unconscious racism: A concept in pursuit of a measure. Annual Review of Sociology, 34, 277–297, 2008.

cxxxv Hutson, Matthew, Implicit Biases Toward Race and Sexuality Have Decreased. Scientific American, April 1, 2019

cxxxvi Blanton, H., & Jaccard, J. Unconscious racism: A concept in pursuit of a measure. Annual Review of Sociology, 34, 277–297, 2008.

cxxxvii Hutson, Matthew, Implicit Biases Toward Race and Sexuality Have Decreased. Scientific American, April 1, 2019

cxxxviii Coutts, Alexander. Racial bias around the world. osf.io, June 24, 2020.

cxxxix Seidman, Gwendolyn. Why do we like people who are similar to us? Psychology Today, December 18, 2018.

cxl Barlett, Tom. Can We Really Measure Implicit Bias? Maybe Not. The Chronicle of Higher Education, January 5, 2017.

cxli Mason, Betsy. Curbing implicit bias: what works and what doesn't. Knowable Magazine, June 4, 2020.

cxlii Riley, Jason. The Race Card has Gone Bust. Wall Street Journal, July 26, 2019.

cxliii Green, Emma. Why do Black Activists Care About Palestine? The Atlantic, August 18, 2016.

cxliv Striple, Zoe. Black Lives Matter hijacked by anti-Semitism. Financial Review, June 24, 2020.

cxlv Cherry, Robert. The Deeply Flawed Racism Index. The National Review, October 29, 2020.

cxlvi Protestors' Anger Justified Even If Actions May Not Be. Monmouth University, 6/2/2020/.

cxlvii Skerry, Peter. Do we really want immigrants to assimilate? Brookings, March/April 2000.

cxlviii The Case against Revolution with Ayaan Hirsi Ali, Hoover Institution, June 25, 2020.

cxlix The Case against Revolution, 2020.

cl Larry Elder: Where's Black Lives Matter when you need them? The Joplin Globe, June 8, 2020.

cli Bertrand, Marianne, Mullainathan, Sendhil. Are Emily and Greg More Employable than Lakisha and Jamal? American Economic Review, 991-1013, September 4, 2004.

clii Turczynski, Bart. Resume Bias: Gender, Names, Ethnicity [2020 Study]. Zety.com, October 13, 2020.

cliii Robinson, Frederick D. The rhetoric of victimization that is paralyzing black America. Chicago Tribune, January 14, 1991.

cliv McWhorter, John. The Dehumanizing Condescension of *White Fragility*. The Atlantic,

July 15, 2020.

[cclv] The new ideology of race. The Economist, July 11-27, 2020

[cclvi] Huffman, Jim. Oregon's Segregated Covid Relief Fund Is Blatantly Unconstitutional. Wall Street Journal, December 4, 2020.

[cclvii] Gonzalez, Mike. For Five Months, BLM Protesters Trashed America's Cities. Heritage.org, November 6, 2020.

[cclviii] Papke, D. Heretics in the Temple: Americans Who Reject the Nation's Legal Faith. NYU Press, 1998.

[cclix] Simpson, B., Willer, R., & Feinberg, M. Does Violent Protest Backfire? Testing a Theory of Public Reactions to Activist Violence. Socius, 2018.

[cclx] Pettigrew, T. F., & Meertens, R. W. Subtle and blatant prejudice in western Europe. European Journal of Social Psychology, 25, 57-75, 1995.

[cclxi] Witt, Will. Are the Police Targeting Unarmed Black Men? PragerU, July 15, 2020. Pettigrew, Thomas. Intergroup Prejudices: its causes and cures. Actualidades en Psicología 22(109):115, February 2011.

[cclxiii] Grzeszczak, Jocelyn. 81% of Black Americans Don't Want Less Police Presence Despite Protests—Some Want More Cops: Poll. Newsweek, August 6, 2020.

[cclxiv] Powell, John, A. University of Arkansas Clinton School of Public Service & Center on Community Philanthropy, 2013.

[cclxv] Horowitz, Juliana, Brown, Anna, Cox, Kiana. The role of race and ethnicity in American's personal lives. Pew Social Trends, April 9, 2019.

[cclxvi] McKenna, Barbara. The color of Black: Professor explores racial identity in college students. Stanford Graduate School of Education, retrieved July 14, 2020.

[cclxvii] Baldwin, J.A. African self-consciousness and the mental health of African-Americans. Journal of BlackStudies,15,177-19, 1984

[cclxviii] Parham, T. A., Cycles of Psychological Nigrescence. The Counseling Psychologist, 17(2), 187–226, 1989.

[cclxix] Sellers, R. M., & Shelton, J. N. The role of racial identity in perceived racial discrimination. Journal of Personality and Social Psychology, 84(5), 1079–1092, 2003.

[cclxx] Michael T. Schmitt & Nyla R. Branscombe. The Meaning and Consequences of Perceived Discrimination in Disadvantaged and Privileged Social Groups, European Review of Social Psychology, 12:1, 167-199, 2002.

[cclxxi] Greenwald, A. G., & Pettigrew, T. F. With malice toward none and charity for some: Ingroup favoritism enables discrimination. American Psychologist, 69(7), 669–684, 2014.

[cclxxii] Police supporters rally to decry Seattle City Council Push to Defund Police. Seattle Times, August 10, 2010.

[cclxxiii] Fryer, Ronald G. An Empirical Analysis of Racial Differences in Police Use of Force. Harvard.edu, July 2017.

[cclxxiv] Fortner, Michael Javen. Hearing what black voices really say about police. City-journal.org, July 5, 2020.

[cclxxv] Axt, J. R., Ebersole, C. E., & Nosek, B. A. An unintentional, robust, and replicable pro-Black bias in social judgment. Social Cognition, 2016.

[cclxxvi] Moss P, Tilly C. Stories Employers Tell: Race, Skill and Hiring in America. New York: Russell Sage Found; 2001.

[cclxxvii] Horowitz, Americans See Advantages.

[cclxxviii] Diversity and inclusion: The reality gap:2017 Human Capital Trends. Deloitte Insights, February 28, 2017.

[cclxxix] Chamorro-Pemuzic, Tomas. Science explains why unconscious bias training won't reduce workplace racism. Here's what will. Fast Company, June 12, 2020.

[cclxxx] Iran: Thousands arbitrarily detained and at risk of torture in chilling post-protest crackdown. Amnesty International, December 16, 2019.

[cclxxxi] Nigeria's Slave Descendants Hope Race Protests Help End Discrimination. VOAnews.com, June 29, 2020.